CHANGING
YOUR EQUATION

Jim & Joanne,
    We hope you always
strive for your own
    Ideal Future !

Ra Boggoski   Dan Pichu

CHANGING
YOUR EQUATION

Moving toward Your
Ideal Future

Roe and Don Polczynski Jr.

CHANGING YOUR EQUATION
MOVING TOWARD YOUR IDEAL FUTURE

Photo credit: Liz Cowie Photography

iUniverse books may be ordered through booksellers or by contacting:

iUniverse
1663 Liberty Drive
Bloomington, IN 47403
www.iuniverse.com
1-800-Authors (1-800-288-4677)

ISBN: 978-1-5320-1120-7 (sc)
ISBN: 978-1-5320-1122-1 (hc)
ISBN: 978-1-5320-1121-4 (e)

Library of Congress Control Number: 2016918733

Print information available on the last page.

iUniverse rev. date: 12/31/2016

To our "fairy godchildren" and others who welcome
our input and advice in their lives, we truly hope
this book leads you to your own ideal future.

To our parents, both in heaven and on earth, and
our close family members and friends, thank you
for your support, inspiration, and love.

Contents

Preface

As we sat on a favorite beach, one we had visited often, a question we had asked so many times came to mind: "When will we reach our ideal future?" We use the phrase *ideal future* as a personal collection of goals, hopes, dreams, and things a person would like to do to live life to its fullest potential. It means living without regret and maximizing all the days of our lives.

In the conversation we were having that day on the beach, our daydreaming thoughts soon blossomed into a full-fledged discussion about our future. We worked hard. We gave back to others. We strove to improve our lives, yet we realized we were still asking that same question: "When do we reach our goals?"

The tough moment came when Don said, "We might not get there."

In a heartbeat, Roe replied, "That's not good enough. I can't accept that."

Finally, the epiphany came: we must either alter the vision of our ideal future or alter ourselves. We realized we had a crucial decision to make and could choose one of two options:

1. Stay on our current path and accept that we would not achieve many of our goals.
2. Change our path in a way that would allow us to obtain more of the components of our ideal future.

It was up to us. Only we could make the choice.

The energy from that epiphany was hard to contain, so we got up and started walking on that beloved beach. Walking always seemed to bring out our best ideas, and those ideas were greatly needed. As the conversation continued, we came to the conclusion that we did not want to change the vision of our ideal future, and so instead we would change ourselves. It was time to cross the line, and there would be no going back. We didn't yet know what was on the other side of the line; we just knew that the status quo was no longer good enough.

With that fresh realization in mind, we stopped and literally drew a line in the sand. Holding hands, counting down, we crossed the line together. It was time to transform, and it needed to be a significant transformation. Crossing that line represented a profound shift in our mind-set. The decision and commitment to change had been made.

As we left our vacation spot and returned home, the development process continued. Our new determination brought with it the inevitable next question: "What do we change?" What could we possibly change? Weren't we doing enough already? No, obviously it wasn't enough. Some of our goals were still too far out of reach.

In grade school math, we all learn that the result of a problem is always the same unless the factors change. As we thought about the goals we wanted to achieve, we realized the same held true when applied to life. Our equation needed to change. We could not move forward toward fulfilling our ideal future unless we changed the factors in our life equation. This, of course, led to the next question: "What is the equation?" At that point, the only thing we were clear on was that we needed to understand this equation before we could set out to change it.

We continued to think about the vision of our ideal future and tried to determine what was preventing us from obtaining it. Was it our current careers, financial issues, past choices, and/or other influencers? The more we thought about it, the clearer it became that these were indeed some of the factors in the life equation. As we refined the idea of what factors could be in a life equation, we knew that many of the details we discussed could be categorized and become factors. This realization was our first major step of change after crossing the line. Our dreams and goals were big, and the only way to turn those dreams into reality was to develop the factors and the equation.

As we thought about the core idea of changing the equation, we realized just how often people ask, "Why can't I have what I want?" without ever knowing the answer. Yet the answer is out there. It is possible to reach the goals, hopes, dreams, and items that make up an ideal future. The first place to start is to take wishes and turn them into actions. In our own lives, we have transformed "We wish we could ..." into a statement of commitment: "This is how we can ..." Everyone can and should make this transformation.

It was this transformation that inspired us to write this book. The growth we experienced after discovering the factors did not mean doing more for ourselves. It meant doing more for others. The primary way we could accomplish this would be to share our experiences. From education to career to life, we have a wealth of knowledge and insight. If you look at our sum, you will see that together we have amassed two master's degrees in business administration and management. We have more than thirty-five years of management and leadership experience, and we have successfully started a business. We've learned from countless leadership books and have had the privilege of working with many excellent mentors, coaches, and consultants. We now have many of the insights we wished others had taught us along the way. We were absolutely convinced we had something important and valuable that needed to be shared. And so we began to use the ideal future equation to develop this book.

We want you to gain clarity as to what makes up your own ideal future and the potential actions that will become your path to it. This book will likely raise your awareness around many elements of life you may have never given much thought. While awareness is essential to the change process, increasing awareness by itself will move you nowhere. Ultimately, this book is about holding yourself accountable for taking action—action that will put you in motion and keep you moving toward your ideal future.

The three main sections of this book reflect the three groups of factors within the equation. These will be explained more in the introduction. Each chapter will focus on an individual factor of the equation so as to build your awareness of essential key points, including assessment tools and recommended actions needed to invoke change. To get the most out of this book, work through one chapter at a time, completing suggested exercises and tools for each chapter in sequence. Along the way, you will read many of our own personal stories.

It is our sincerest hope that you, and all our readers, will use this book as a road map for changing your equation to reach your ideal future.

Introduction

It is not in the stars to hold our destiny but in ourselves.
—*William Shakespeare*

Change does not happen by magic. It isn't something someone else can do for you, nor can you do it for another. The change in mind-set needed to make any change means you must be your own personal leader. The goal is to leave the mind-set of "just getting by" behind. This is the time to take the helm of your life and navigate the journey to your ideal future.

Personal Leadership

- According to Joelle K. Jay, PhD: "Personal leadership is the leadership of the self. It is the ability to define a direction for your leadership and life, and to move in that direction with consistency and clarity."

While you are leading yourself toward change, remember that you don't have to go it alone and are not without resources to help along the way. The change you need doesn't mean you have to totally create the way you should go or the methods you should use. Others have successfully made changes, and their lessons will be your guide. As unique as we may all seem, we are far more alike than we are different. In learning from each other, we can learn more about ourselves. Transforming your life is a challenging-enough process as it is; why not use knowledge gained from others to help along the way?

For your first shift in mind-set, understand that developing yourself doesn't have to be a painful process. It may not be easy at times, but it should not be something that is so agonizing that you don't go any further. As humans, we try to be so independent, even taking great pride at times in going it alone. However, when we are so determined to learn on our own, we often experience pain and its aftereffects. Rather than admit that we should have listened, learned, or asked for help, we wear the pain like a badge of honor, as if to say, "I learned it the hard way, so can you." Why is this so necessary for our self-worth? Change is difficult enough. Do you really want to add pain to the process?

Our intent for you is to gain insight into the changes you need and want in your life—insight we wish more people had helped us gain along the way. The learning principles in this book are designed to help you avoid needless painful experiences. Implementing change in your life—the change required to fulfill your dreams and aspirations—should be a journey of discovery and enjoyment. While this journey should be savored, and our experiences can help you do that, remember that getting through these changes will require your own personal accountability, action, and effort. There is no magic potion. You cannot just make a wish on a star and reach your ideal future.

Hopes and dreams, however, will certainly help, and there *is* a secret formula for bringing the elements of the change process to light. We have developed an equation to help others understand the aspects of their lives they can and should change.

So here goes. Here is our formula for you to use in changing your equation:

This formula has three factors, different yet related to your ideal future. Certainly the vision of an ideal future will vary from person to person, but these three basic factors are universal to everyone.

Our ideal future isn't so much a destination as a journey made up of every future day in our lives. We will never wake up one morning and exclaim, "We're there. We've reached our ideal future!" No, the ideal future is always more about making choices that create a path toward living life to our fullest potential—maximizing fulfillment and simultaneously minimizing regret. It means finding your path, owning it, and leading the way. You will no longer accept a path full of ifs and maybes. Your ideal future is far too important to leave to chance or for others to determine its outcome. Our decision was to take full ownership of our path to the ideal future and everything that it would bring to our lives.

An ideal future is a collection of dreams, goals, and wishes that come to fruition. An ideal future realized is a life lived to full potential. It is the ability to look back at your life with satisfaction and meaning. Failure to obtain your ideal future leads to a life full of regrets. In embracing the concept of an ideal future, you're refusing to accept those regrets. Instead, you're using short-term and long-term goals to create your vision of the major items you want to accomplish in your lifetime. It is time to manage the factors to obtain the ideal future.

▓ Life Elements

Life elements make up the first factor in our equation because they form the foundation of who we are. They are our core, and they are universal. Everyone has them. Collectively, they constitute where we are today—the starting point. Relationships, values and ethics, education, finances, and career are some of the elements that define who you are today.

We all need this higher level of understanding before we can set a course to where we want to go—that destination being our ideal future. By embracing the need to inventory where you stand in life, your life elements will come into sharper focus. Then you will be ready to move forward toward implementing the changes needed to reach your ideal future.

▓ Realities

The next set of factors in our ideal future equation are those comprising our realities. These include the reality of you as a person, the reality of others around you, and the reality of a leader's world. They are the real truths that make up our lives. Using personal leadership to manage your equation and reach the ideal future means you must have a realistic perspective of your world and what is truly achievable. Some will say you can do anything you want as long as you set your mind to it. While we are absolutely against shutting people down, in developing this equation the need for a real understanding of what is achievable becomes paramount to obtaining an ideal future.

It's fine to have out-of-this-world hopes and dreams, but you can't let them become a wild fantasy that distorts the reality of who you are and what is actually achievable. Your ideal future needs to be rooted in reality, not fantasy. This distortion is more common than you may think. In such a media-focused culture, it is easy to be led away from the truth in our lives. For example, how many talent shows are shown, and just how few people have true, uniquely gifted talent? While we might not be one of those few, we do have our own talents that are uniquely our own. We need to be aware of our strengths—and yes, our limitations.

The reality factor helps us capitalize on our individual talents instead of trying to capture the talents of others. Chasing the fantasy will not bring any of us to our ideal future, no matter how hard we try. In the end, we want to find our purpose or accurately see our true selves, and we have to acknowledge and understand just how much reality impacts our ideal future.

▮ Change Agents

The final set of factors in our ideal future equation is our change agents. These are the elements we can or should change—we just may not know how to change them or even be aware of their existence. When we get trapped in things like financial limitations, past experiences, the inability to ask for help, the person we try to portray to others, the failure to create opportunities for ourselves, the hopelessness of being unable to forgive, and the inability to realize that we need to believe and have beliefs, we are actually creating roadblocks—self-imposed roadblocks. These roadblocks cause the agents of change to become invisible. Even though they are all around us, we become blind to what is changeable.

The epiphany in all of this is that a slight change of perspective will make them visible and allow us to harness their incredible power to create change. Our goal is to help you clear self-imposed roadblocks, make the invisible visible, and transform yourself from powerless to powerful so that your change agents become actionable. You can then accelerate the pace of change and achieve more than you ever imagined. The distant ideal future won't be so distant anymore. What once seemed so far away is now at your fingertips.

▨ Move into Action: Envisioning Your Ideal Future

Use this tool to begin to develop your ideal future. Begin by answering these questions, and keep refining your answers as you progress through this book. Use this page or create a journal of your own. It doesn't matter as long as it is a list you can refer back to. Remember—an ideal future is ever evolving, so make sure you keep updating and refining it as you move forward on your life's journey.

In this column, list your goals, hopes, dreams, or anything you think will help you live life to its fullest potential.	Use this column to answer the question, "Why is this important?"	In this column, answer the question, "What difference or value will it bring to my life?"	Answer this final question over time: "How does the life equation need to be used to make this possible?"

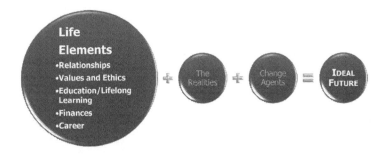

Section 1
LIFE ELEMENTS

In thinking about how we got here, how we became who we are, and how it influences our ideal future, we have to look at the beliefs, experiences, and situations that have brought us to this moment. They are our personal collection of life elements, and they are at the core of our equation. In order to reach your ideal future, you must take stock and learn about your own life elements. This first section will take you on that learning journey.

The first stop is to evaluate your relationships, where you will begin to understand who is helping you to move forward and who might be holding you back. Next come values and ethics—your core approach to conducting your life and executing those choices. From there we delve into your education and examine the need to continue learning throughout your lifetime. Financial health is a life element that everyone has but not everyone understands. The final chapter in this section looks at how your career is a launchpad toward your ideal future.

At the end of each chapter, you will find a tool to assess the various concepts associated with your life elements. The collection of these tools will lead to a better awareness of your personal situation and how it affects your equation.

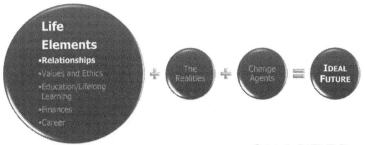

CHAPTER 1

Relationships

Our relationships either help us to reach our ideal future or hold us back. In developing your personal leadership to change your equation, you must develop the ability to acknowledge, accept, and act on the difference between who is really adding value to your life factors and who is sucking the life out of you. It is time to foster positive interactions and eliminate those who wear you down.

Think of it this way: Have you ever seen kids at the mall who are determined to go up the down escalator? They climb and climb and end up in the same place. Then the trouble begins. Older folks yell at them. Their parents yell at them. Security yells at them. What seemed like fun turns out to be a lot of wasted energy, a lot of effort, and no forward progress. If they had just gotten on the escalator that was moving in the direction they wanted to go, they would have gotten there with far less effort and far fewer problems.

Our relationships are like that escalator. They can either move us forward or hold us back. Which would you prefer?

Of course, since you're reading this book, we assume you want to move forward. In our approach to changing your relationship life factor, there are three key concepts: generosity and goodwill, reflection, and leadership. As you read through these concepts in detail, take some time to think about your current relationships. Keep the escalator in mind. Are your relationships moving you closer to your ideal future or holding you back?

Generosity

• According to Merriam-Webster's dictionary, generosity is "the quality of being kind, understanding, and not selfish ... willingness to give money and other valuable things to others."

Concept #1: Generosity and Goodwill

Consider your best relationships. What makes them great? Chances are these are the relationships you've given the most to—the most time, the most energy, the most dedication. The irony is that our best relationships are that way because of what we give to them, not what we expect to receive. Anything we do receive is the result of our generosity and should not be an expectation. The more we give, the more we likely receive. If we want to receive more, we must give more.

This cycle of generosity leads to the creation of relationship goodwill—mutually shared care, compassion, and concern. Others want to help you in return for the generosity you showed them. You then want to help the other person for helping you, and so on and so on. This is the foundation of great friendships, business teams, and even romantic partnerships.

The best part is that this doesn't always have to start with a big, lavish act. It may begin with a little gesture. Perhaps your generosity was an act of kindness or the giving of a gift. To you, it may have seemed very small, but you don't know how much it was valued by the recipient. That value may be so great that the other person has a desire to act with generosity in return. One small good deed leads to another.

Relationship Tip

Little things really do count! It is often more important to do many small acts of kindness than one large gesture. Remember people's birthdays, ask about their families, or even invite them out for a cup of coffee if life seems to be a struggle for them. Showing your care, compassion, and concern will open the door for them to do the same. Be kind and make sure you respond in kind.

In our day-to-day interactions with others, we have a natural tendency to create and utilize goodwill without ever giving it much thought. For example, if a teammate was having trouble with a project, you might have stepped in to help him or her complete it. Those you help in this way are grateful and tell you to let them know if they can ever help you out. At some point, if you need help, who are you going to ask? Your first thought will probably go to your teammate or someone else you've done favors for in the past who has responded with gratitude. The goodwill cycle was previously established and can be easily used.

In relationships, goodwill is an asset, potentially a very valuable one. In order to obtain your ideal future, you will have to rely on your past generosity and the established circle of goodwill. When you do something for someone or give someone a gift without expectation of receiving anything in return, it likely gives you a positive feeling. That is a great reaction, isn't it? The way we get more of it is to do more good deeds and give more gifts.

Now turn the situation around 180 degrees. Consider how other people feel when they help you or give you a gift. They enjoy that same great positive feeling. Allowing others to repay some of that goodwill isn't being selfish. In some regards, it's being downright generous. It is allowing others to have that same experience. We have to allow for the repayment of goodwill to perpetuate the cycle. One-sided relationships don't maximize value and are destined to die.

> *When your dream is bigger than you are, you*
> *have two choices: give up or get help.*
> *—John C. Maxwell*

To leverage goodwill and generosity, you need to be open to the idea that others actually want to help you get what you want out of life. They want to assist you for your sake and their own. Let them. Think about how much relationship goodwill you have and with whom you have it. This is likely a difficult question. Yet we're going to ask you to give it considerable thought. Where among your relationships have you been generous and created goodwill? How might that person want to assist you in obtaining your ideal future? With this approach, you are fully using the power of the cycle of generosity.

However, there is an issue if the cycle is not complete. When generosity only goes one way, it shows a darker side: greed. If generosity is the great relationship-builder and creator of goodwill, then greed is the great relationship-destroyer and creator of ill will. This is best illustrated in what we call "the weighty friend."

We'll bet you have or have had at least one friend in your life who leaves you feeling drained. After finishing a conversation, you feel the weight of all the issues that person just dumped on you. He or she took your attention and energy and offered little or nothing in return. You feel anxious and stressed rather than joyful and happy. Such individuals are actually being greedy. They are hoarding all the goodwill in the relationship and not sharing any with you.

The irony is you may really like this person. He or she might be funny, charming, or seemingly a good person to have your back. At first, you jumped at the chance to help. Your friend was in crisis, and only you could save the day. Yet over time, you recognize the pattern. What you have created, what you have allowed to develop, is a one-way street. These people are always in need and expect you to be sympathetic to whatever problems they have. Their problems become your problems. The weight of this baggage builds and builds. Instead of looking forward to the next encounter, you start dreading it, fearing what issue is about to be dumped on you this time.

Sound familiar? This is such a common problem. We start off with good intentions. We start by being generous with ourselves and building goodwill. What we didn't do was make sure it was a complete circle. We didn't ensure that our own needs were being met along the way. The moral of the story is that you cannot become the weighty friend, nor should you hang on to the weighty friend. Find the balance between give and take.

Greed takes many forms that result in ill will. This ill will kills relationships and creates great liability in life. Liabilities will certainly stand in the way of obtaining your ideal future. Our next concept, reflection, can help you see where relationships like this are lurking.

Concept #2: Reflection

Quick, write down the names of the five people you spend the most time with in your life. Now think about this: If you tell us a little about each of them, we'll know a lot about you. You are a reflection of those you're closest to. This is directly in line with the adage from Jim Rohn that you're the average of the five people who surround you. What might we be able to discern about you based on these five people? We could likely make some good guesses about your level of wealth, educational background, type of career, interests, hobbies, and even general demeanor, including how positive or negative you tend to be. In general, your life is likely headed in the same direction as those five other people.

How does that make you feel? Are you proud of that average? The answer to those two questions probably depends on whether or not you are lifted up by that average or pulled down by it. In developing your relationships so as to obtain your ideal future, you can't resist the notion that your friends define who you are.

While we are often blind to the impact our friends have on us, it can be can easy to see the forces in action on others around us. We can see their reflection, but we cannot see our own. Be assured your reflection is visible. Those around you see it quite clearly too.

In one of our early mentorship roles, we were mentoring a young woman we'll call Anne. She was really struggling with negativity and could not maintain a positive outlook on her work and her life. The sky was always falling. Everything was horrible, and she had no future. Anne was confused and couldn't grasp where the negativity was coming from. She didn't know who or what to believe. Everything reflected poorly, even though that was not the true picture.

We knew Anne had a very close business friend who was feeding her continual negativity. No matter what positive event happened, this friend would convince Anne it was an absolute negative. When we raised this situation with Anne, she insisted that this friend was a great asset to her life and that no such negativity existed. Anne adamantly maintained this thinking for a long time. We would no sooner plant a positive thought than Anne would return with a negative outlook. We could see the reflection of Anne's friend in her.

We continued to press forward. Though we made some progress, there were still times when she would relapse into negativity. It was a constant battle. Then one day, life changed. Anne's friend left the area and easily left her behind. The realization hit full force. Free from her friend, Anne realized the tremendous negative influence she had been under. Almost immediately, that invisible negative pull became clearly visible. Anne was stunned that for years she could not see the reflection. Her life changed dramatically and positively once this negative pull ended.

Anne's story is repeated time and time again. Failure to see the reflection of invisible forces around you is something we all need to be aware of. How do we see what is invisible to our own eyes? We need to allow ourselves to see the situation through the eyes of others, for they can often see these forces that are pushing and pulling on us clearly. There is another old saying: "You can choose your friends, but you can't choose your family." Our advice is to choose friends carefully, because they just might become a big part of your reflection.

Your relationships exert powerful influences in your life. Initiate positive relationships that will propel you forward. Step away from the negative relationships that are pulling you backward and keeping you from moving toward the attainment of your full potential.

▨ Concept #3: Leadership

Leadership is often considered to be a relationship among at least two people. There exists a relationship between every leader and each of his or her followers. But the most important relationship you have is the one with yourself. Simply put, changing your equation has a lot to do with leading yourself.

There is an old saying, "Do as I say, not as I do." That generally is a bad mind-set for leading yourself. Your number-one responsibility in leading yourself is to model the way. Would you follow people who didn't walk their own talk? Not too likely, is it? Walking your own talk is essential to leading yourself. Apply the same principles of leadership that instill confidence and the desire of others to follow you. These principles include honesty, integrity, drive, gratitude, and generosity—all aspects of great leadership that we must first apply to ourselves.

When you neglect yourself, you become a victim of yourself. This takes many forms, yet all lead to one common outcome: regret. If you neglect your health, education, finances, career, or relationships, you'll end up regretting it. Who is responsible? You and you alone. There is no one else to blame. It is up to you to get to the gym, or go back to school, or save for whatever it is you want, or find ways to do better at work, or find joy in others. Only you know what you want, what is best for you, and how to obtain it. If you have not accepted the responsibility and accountability to lead your own life, stop whatever you're doing and make this your first priority. Acknowledge your responsibility, accept the role as leader of your life, and act on the changes that will bring you to your ideal future.

■ Move into Action: Your Relationships

Use this tool to assess your relationships. Think of the top five people you're closest to; the goal here is to determine if each of them is a positive or negative influencer. Make sure your answers are a true depiction of the person. Once you have completed this, consider how to move forward with those relationships.

List your top five people in this column	How much generosity and goodwill do you share with each other?	Does this person add weight to your life or lift you up?	What would your reflection look like without this person?	Looking at all of your previous answers, is this person a positive or negative influencer?
1.				
2.				
3.				
4.				
5.				

11

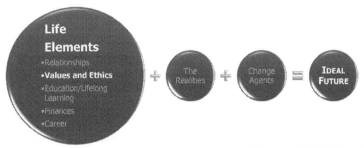

CHAPTER 2

Values and Ethics

Put yourself in this scenario: A person approaches you on the street and offers you a large, life-changing sum of money if you can quickly answer two personal questions. No strings attached. Provide the answers, and the money is yours. If you can't do it, the person will just take the money and try to find someone else. The only rules are that there is no hesitation allowed—no "ums" or "I don't knows"—and taking time to think isn't allowed either. Your answers must be clear, concise, and quickly stated. Sounds like it's at least worth a shot, right? After all, it is a life-changing amount of money. You should be able to do this, shouldn't you?

Here are the questions: Declare your values and state your ethics. All you have to do is succinctly list what you value the most, describe the standards you hold yourself and others to, and explain how you choose to act toward people. Could you do it? Does your mind go blank? Would you be able to find the right words in that brief moment?

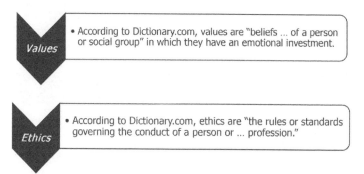

Values
• According to Dictionary.com, values are "beliefs ... of a person or social group" in which they have an emotional investment.

Ethics
• According to Dictionary.com, ethics are "the rules or standards governing the conduct of a person or ... profession."

The sad truth is that many people, maybe yourself included, couldn't do it. The answers would not come very quickly or without much thought. Because the values and ethics that form your personal code of conduct may be hard to describe, they can be thought of as the invisible characteristics that affect your equation. You know they are within, yet you rarely make a conscientious effort to make them visible.

The values and ethics in your personal code of conduct affect you every day, even when you least expect it, and you need to know what that code is so you can develop and refine it. Stating your values and ethics shouldn't be a struggle. Let's take it one step further: put yourself in the following scenarios with the same rules of quickly and succinctly providing your answers:

1. A manager approaches you at work and offers you a chance to earn a very large amount of money, free and clear of taxes, by selling goods to a customer on the side. The manager swears to you that no one will ever find out.
2. You approach an ATM in a grocery store and find two hundred dollars sitting in the cash dispenser. No one is around; it was just left there.
3. During an interview for a job you really need, you're asked if you could handle meeting the numbers, however unrealistic they may be and regardless of the human toll.

Three different scenarios—all of which have happened in real life. The pressure is mounting. You have a split second to decide. What do you do? Are you able to quickly and succinctly act the way you really want to in these situations? Do you hesitate and frantically try to figure out how to respond? Worse yet, do you act quickly and later regret your hasty choices?

Some of these scenarios could be career-ending and even illegal. They would take you very far off the path to your ideal future. These real scenarios happen more than you may realize. Would you be prepared to respond?

Your personal code of conduct is your protection against situations like those described above. If your code is your shield, once it is cracked it is hard to repair. The guilt, shame, and consequences of your actions take hold. In an instant, you're forced to decide if you can look at yourself in the mirror tomorrow. Because your personal code of conduct affects your life equation, let's look at ways to make your ethics and values visible.

It's not hard to make decisions when you know what your values are.
—Roy E. Disney

Clearly Define Your Values and Ethics

In developing your personal leadership and striving for your ideal future, you must have complete clarity about your code of conduct and the values and ethics that shape your experiences. Just think about the internal battles you've had over these situations and how much stress you went through. How often have you mentally beaten yourself up because your actions were out of line with your true beliefs? Have you ever wished you could go back in time and change the outcome?

Now think about it from a different perspective. What if you were prepared to handle such situations before they even happened? There would be no second-guessing. No struggle. No stress. No need to go back in time. Your values and ethics would be clearly visible. You would know them and be ready for battle. This is the mind-set you need in order to develop your personal leadership, and there is no reason you can't or shouldn't adopt this perspective. The goal now is to become closer to this positive outcome and use it to help obtain your ideal future.

Going back to the person on the street and the questions about your values and ethics, how can they be defined? The reality is, we are surrounded by people behaving very badly. The focus is placed on what people do for a living and how much money they make rather than how they live their life. When we put all of our attention on the end career result, we lose the understanding of how we should get ourselves there. More importantly, we lose the perspective of how we impact others along the way. These gaps need to be narrowed.

The first step to narrowing these gaps is to make a list of who and what you value most. This is not a chance to list your material possessions; it is a chance to inventory your emotional possessions. Start with what comes easily to your mind when thinking about what is important to you, what you hold dear, and how you want to live your life. It may be your family connections, your relationship with God, or how you interact with the world around you. In this list, you're focusing on the bigger picture of your life. In all of this, there are no right or wrong answers as long as you're completely honest with yourself.

In the next phase of developing the list, focus on your interactions in the world around you. Think about those qualities that irk you—those things you despise in others. These qualities may be found in your business and personal relationships. They may even come from outside influencers, such as the media, entertainment, and political and public figures. It doesn't matter who they come from; it just matters that you find them unacceptable and don't want them in your world. For example, if you hate when you catch someone lying, make a note that you value honesty. If it really bothers you when you see a supervisor stealing someone else's glory, note the value you place on letting other people have a chance to succeed. Learn more about yourself by observing the world around you.

Now it is time to look deeply at your own interactions. Think about the times you felt valued and were happy in your situation. It also works when you think about how you have affected and influenced others in a positive way. In more simple terms, you are applying the Golden Rule. You want to treat others as you want to be treated. To ensure that you're successful, you are going to define what the Golden Rule means to you.

An example of this may be found in a past supervisor. Perhaps she worked with you to help you find your best career path, even though it meant that you were moving on. You were affected and influenced by the value she placed on nurturing others. Now it may become a value that you would like to pay forward. Focus on these interactions, these examples of the Golden Rule, and you will find a treasure trove of personal values. Once again, it is your list, and you're the one who will be making it visible. Make sure it is truly in line with the person you strive to be and the life you want to live.

▨ Own Your Values and Ethics

There is a final step in the creation of your list of values and ethics. By transforming your values into actionable deeds, you're transforming them into your ethics. You must be ethical in living up to the values you have set. If you value honesty and the importance of helping others, then ethically you must turn in the ATM money, for example. There are no ifs, ands, or buts. Ethics should serve as a guide keeping you pointed in the direction you want to go. To complete this step, take all the values and turn them into actionable statements. If one of your values is honesty, an ethical action statement might be, "I will strive to be truthful and act with integrity in all of my interactions."

What if you didn't turn in that ATM money, even though you say you value honesty? In that split second, you go against what you value. You need the money, so you keep it and you justify it with the expression, "Finders keepers, losers weepers." But those of us who value honesty know better. If we don't act in line with our values, the expression turns into, "Finders keepers, finders regret." We get trapped in a deteriorating cycle of remorse. After we leave, thoughts of the poor "loser weeper" swirl in our mind. That might have been someone's grocery money for the week. That might have paid for someone's day care. Oh no, maybe that was needed for medicine. The regret builds, and our personal integrity sinks.

Regret is a feeling that rarely works out very well. Without integrity, we are without our internal guide. As time passes, we dwell on the regret and feel our own personal betrayal for those situations which we have caused to go badly.

As bad as the ATM scenario is, it keeps happening because we didn't prepare ourselves to handle it correctly the first time, so we fell into a trap of bad behavior. We took the money. We already have the guilt of being a "bad person," so what stops us from taking something else—especially if the opportunity presents itself? It becomes easier and easier to say, "I am going to hell anyway, so I might as well go for it." By not actively understanding and ethically living by our values, we create an unbalanced equation. We aren't living the life we want to live. This area has to be in alignment before we can reach our ideal future.

Always remember values and ethics are your core, your foundation. They need to be visible. You are transforming your personal values into actions within your world, and no one or nothing should stop you. The problems of the past have arisen because you have not proactively managed the nonnegotiables in your life. The nonnegotiables are those values and ethics that matter most and make you who you are. They are rock solid, and you do not want to be swayed from them. You won't be swayed from them. They will help you obtain your ideal future.

Visibility Tip

To truly make the invisible visible, share your values and ethics with others. Discuss your list with those closest to you and carefully consider their honest feedback. This is a great way to engage others while holding yourself more accountable for your own actions.

In the section that follows, you will find an example of our own personal values list and how we translated it into our personal ethics. Use it as a guide to forming your own list. Encourage your family to do the same. It won't take long; ours was completed in less than thirty minutes. Truly, we could have answered the person on the street, and you should be able to as well. Take the guidance from above and just make the invisible visible. This visibility is not only for yourself right now, it's also a solid layer in the foundation of your ideal future.

Our Personal Values and Ethics

Here are our results from the values and ethics exercise. While the results were not at all surprising to us, the clarity that we gained was one of the best uses of thirty minutes we've experienced. Do we value many more things in life? Sure we do. These are our core values or the foundation upon which all else is built.

Now, let's turn those values into action statements of our ethics.

This exercise is deceptively simple in relation to the value of the results. Any builder will tell you that a structure is only as good as its foundation. Without understanding the foundation of your life, it is difficult to build much of anything that will stand the test of time.

Move into Action: Make the Invisible Visible

Use this tool to create a list of your values. Use as many or as few of the lines as you need. Once you have your values set, create action statements that define your ethics. Make sure you live by them and allow them to be visible.

List Your Most Important Values	
1.	6.
2.	7.
3.	8.
4.	9.
5.	10.

11.	16.
12.	17.
13.	18.
14.	19.
15.	20.

Turn Your Values into Statements of Ethics

CHAPTER 3

Education and Lifelong Learning

When you graduated from high school, it was time to determine where to go next. There were so many roads to choose. They all had the appeal that the first taste of freedom and impending adulthood promises. Which road did you take? Did you choose college, military/public service, a trade school, or going right to work? It is very likely the decisions you made are not the ones that are going to lead to your ideal future. Somewhere along the way, what you thought you wanted turned out to be far from what you needed now. When you made your choice, did you really understand the impact it would have on your future?

Regardless of the choice made then, there are always opportunities to grow and learn something new. To develop personal leadership, you must establish patterns and habits for yourself through many forms of learning. You have to come into alignment, plan for the ceiling, and embrace lifelong learning. You have to find what works for you and what will help to fulfill your vision of an ideal future.

> **Education Tip**
>
> Be brave and try different things. Community colleges and other educational institutions often have a variety of classes for adults who want to expand their knowledge base. Go to their websites, look at the catalogs when they come in the mail, or contact the institution directly to learn more. Taking a few of these classes can open doors to your future that you didn't even know existed.

Alignment

At some point in life, the education we have may fail to align with the goals for our ideal future. Some start down a path in college that progresses into a lifelong career. Most of us, though, wake up one day and realize our education doesn't support where we want to go or what we want to do in life. We come to the frightening realization that we are now in a state of misalignment. This happens in so many ways, and the cause can be pinpointed to change or the fear of it.

For team members who may not have a formal business degree, or any degree at all, the thought of returning to college can be paralyzing. They imagine the rejection letters because they don't have the right undergraduate studies or were poor students in high school. They refuse to even consider the possibilities more education might hold. The rationalization begins: There isn't anything more they could possibly learn from a book that they haven't experienced on the job. Why waste all that time and money when there is real work to be done?

This holds true for many adults who know they need any type of college education, whether it is going for an MBA or just starting with an associate's degree. They know it is exactly what they need, yet they cannot seem to take the first steps toward attempting it. They choose to remain in a state of misalignment.

What if you continue to try to move forward in your life even though you're misaligned? It isn't likely to be a pleasant experience. You can try to proceed, but the forces that caused you to get misaligned are likely to continue and make the situation worse over time.

Have you ever driven a car where the wheels are out of alignment? The car may shudder, vibrate, and wander while driving, making it nearly impossible to drive a straight line. If left uncorrected, alignment issues worsen, and soon you have a vehicle that is practically undriveable. The lack of alignment takes a toll on other aspects of your vehicle as well. Tires wear out and other mechanical issues crop up. The problem doesn't simply go away. However, once corrective action is taken and proper alignment is restored, you quickly realize what a huge difference it makes. The car is easier to handle, and the drive is much more enjoyable.

When our education gets out of alignment with our ability to reach our goals, the feelings are strikingly similar. It is stressful to live a life that is misaligned. How could it not be? We want to go in a straight line, we want to reach our goals in a straight line, but we can't. Even though we can park a car that doesn't drive well, we can't just park our lives. There really is only one practical solution: get back into alignment.

When thinking about getting your education and goals into alignment, what feelings have you experienced? Dread? Nervousness? Inability to think about it without a sense of panic? Here is the real secret: those feelings are roadblocks, and they are self-inflicted. You can get back into alignment.

Remember your education is a life element you have control over. It just requires action to change. As that high school student or young adult, you may not have made the best choices. Don't worry! You don't have to live with them forever. It does takes courage to face these past decisions. You must embrace the vulnerability of admitting that while you know your job, you need a more expanded knowledge base. It will definitely take effort—a lot of effort—as well as time and resources to go back to school. Stop putting up self-inflicted barriers. If it needs to be done, do it. You can and should change this element of your equation.

One of the great outcomes in achieving alignment in your education is becoming free—free of your past choices, free to once again feel the rush of pushing yourself in new directions, and free to achieve your ideal future.

■ Hitting Your Head

At times, the problem isn't misalignment, it is just running out of road, so to speak. You had the appropriate education for your current role. After graduating college, you were able to build a nice career in your chosen field of study. Through excelling at your job function, you receive promotion after promotion. Then it happens: the promotions become fewer and farther between. There are more talented people coming through the ranks. They have higher levels of education and more developed skill sets. They are advancing as you once did, and you find yourself stuck.

In this case, you have reached a somewhat different type of roadblock. The education and skill sets that have served you so well up to this point just won't let you go any further. There is no next level or promotion. You are done climbing the ladder and have just hit your head on what may have been an invisible ceiling. For some, especially those closer to retirement, this is acceptable, which is completely understandable. Not everyone wants to continually push forward, and that is fine.

The rest of us, however, face an education gap that is similar to misalignment, and the realization is unpleasant. We need to achieve more to reach our ideal future. We are used to growing, and all of a sudden we are done. We never saw the ceiling, and frustration has set in.

Has this happened to you? Have you gone as far as you can, and you're suddenly at a standstill? Here is the secret: that ceiling should have been no surprise. Being aware of what it is required to take the next step forward in your career is your responsibility. Only you know your ideal future, and it is up to you to use your personal leadership to get there. Knowing where your career is taking you is often a neglected responsibility. Perhaps you thought it was up to your employer to tell you what was in store. Maybe you thought you could make it to the next level on your experience alone. It could be that it never even occurred to you that you should care. Whatever the situation, you're hitting your head on a ceiling and won't be able to reach your ideal future. There is good news, though, as this is both avoidable and correctable.

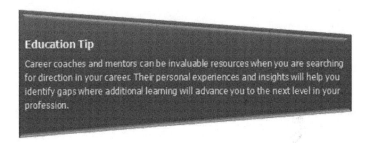

Education Tip

Career coaches and mentors can be invaluable resources when you are searching for direction in your career. Their personal experiences and insights will help you identify gaps where additional learning will advance you to the next level in your profession.

Obviously, avoiding the ceiling in the first place would be ideal. The old saying is that "an ounce of prevention is worth a pound of cure." Prevention simply amounts to being proactive. Don't wait for someone else to make it happen; prepare for it and make it happen yourself. How can you do that? Well, there are a couple of things. First, you must get a clear understanding of the requirements, education, and skill sets required to allow you to grow to the next level in your career. Second, honestly assess whether you possess them. Ultimately, your employer will decide whether you meet those qualifications—and just meeting the qualifications may not be enough. The questions you need to ask yourself are, "Is this what I really want?" and "Am I the best person available to fill the desired position?"

We will assume that it is what you really want and yes, it is likely others either in your organization or external to your organization want the same position. Your goal is take the question away. It is not, are you really the best candidate? It needs to become clear that you are the best candidate. If you aren't chosen or you determine you really don't want that position, it is up to you to research and reflect as to what is in your best interest.

What happens if you didn't avoid the ceiling and you must now redirect yourself? Where can and should you begin to correct your course? First, it is a good time to assess where your career could lead. You are matching what you want with what is possible. If the position you wanted isn't available to you, you must determine where you're going next. There might be one alternative, or there might be several. The key is to understand all of them and how they can help or hinder your arrival at your ideal future.

This assessment phase may mean you have open, difficult conversations with your supervisor and other leaders within your organization. This is also a great time to turn to your trusted mentors. In these conversations, you must identify the skill sets needed for the available alternatives.

In the Move into Action tool at the end of this chapter, you will have a starting point to answer these questions: what do you have, what do you need, and what can you correct? After the assessments and identifications are done, the final step is to take the corrective action. This is the phase in which you acquire the education and skills you're lacking. There are no shortcuts. Whether it is paid for by your employer or not, you must find a way. If you don't, consider the ceiling to be permanent. Only you can remove it.

*Knowledge is exploding, so you need to commit
yourself to a plan for lifelong learning.*
—Don Topscott

▨ Lifelong Learning

Even with a plan in place to avoid the ceiling, and even if you
return to school to get additional education, your ideal future
means there is no end to learning. In college or any learning
institution, there is one goal in mind: to reach the end and
graduate. That mind-set works for a structured education but it
doesn't work for the whole of our lifetime. At no point are we
pronounced graduates of life. We cannot think we have reached
the end of our learning and expect we will just arrive at our ideal
future.

Lifelong learning is just a habit to form. It doesn't matter what
you learn, how you learn it, or why you learn it, as long as this
habit of learning ties to your ideal future goals. Tying it to your
goals will help you be ready to act and to see the opportunities to
learn something that moves you toward your goals.

The habits we form—the good ones, that is—usually grow
out of something we enjoy and feel fulfilled by in some way. The
goal in forming a habit of learning is to discover what works best
for you. As much as we are the same, we do have different ways
of learning. Embracing these differences can lead us to develop
unique lifelong learning methods for ourselves.

Roe's learning plan is less formal. She is usually very aware of
what is going on around her and is constantly analyzing what can
be learned from various situations. This serves her very well in her
business coaching, as she is able to quickly learn from others and
transmit that knowledge to her clients. Don's learning plan, on the
other hand, is very formal and scholarly. He sets annual learning
goals through a planning system and works toward the items on

his list. The approaches are very different, but their success in embracing the opportunity to learn is the same. The approach you take isn't important; what you need to focus on is how best to establish the habit for yourself and look forward to doing it.

In terms of life elements, education is one of the most fixed, yet fixable. No amount of hoping, wishing, or luck will change it. Whether it is bringing yourself into alignment, removing the ceiling, or forming a habit of learning, the only thing that can change the education element is action and a willingness to be open to the possibilities education and lifelong learning have to offer.

▧ Move into Action: Alignment Tool for Education / Lifelong Learning

Use this tool to check the alignment of your educational past and the need for lifelong learning moving forward.

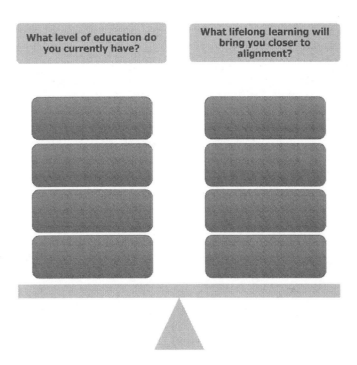

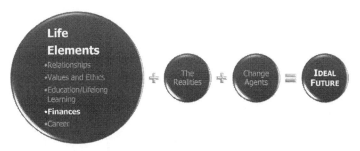

CHAPTER 4

Your Finances

It seems like there is always something keeping you from getting ahead. It may be a medical bill, a car repair, an unexpected home improvement, or any other unforeseen expense. The financial balancing act takes so much time and energy. The stress builds and builds, and you find yourself wishing for more money. If you had more, then you really wouldn't have to worry.

Is more money really the answer, though? Would it take all of your worries away? It might be a temporary fix, especially when those payment due dates are looming. You might even think it is more than temporary, and more money would solve all of your problems. In most cases, however, money isn't the ultimate answer. The majority of people will have to make do with what they have or what they can realistically expect. While you can have a goal of accumulating all the money you could ever want, this goal is often overly lofty and rarely obtainable, leading to disappointment and financial dysfunction. The ultimate goal needs to be creating a leadership approach to your personal financial element.

Financial leadership is understanding you are striving to have all you need, not all you want. There is a big difference between needs and wants. In developing this approach, we are raising personal leadership to a new level. People have to acknowledge where they stand financially today, accept the responsibility for putting themselves in this position, and act on the changes needed to reach their ideal future.

Achieving financial health doesn't mean you have to be rich to be happy. It helps you to know what your financial situation truly is so you can balance the trade-offs involved in making one decision over another. Think of this piece of the equation as developing a path to a better balance between what you need, what you want, and what is realistically possible. Your personal leadership in this area shows you the changes you need to make to reach your ideal future. In the following sections, we'll investigate the idea of savings and spending to help you develop this aspect of personal leadership.

> **Financial Tip**
>
> If you ever wonder where your moneys goes, track it. As tough as it may be, be honest with yourself and note everything you spend, from a postage stamp to your loan payments. Once you have captured this knowledge, you will have a more accurate picture of just what you spend your money on.

Your Piggy Bank

One of the common gifts given to young children is a piggy bank. We all know what a piggy bank is and what it is for. Most of us came to this understanding at a very early age, and it was a very important piece of learning—that this thing called "money" is really important. Ask children how much money is in their piggy bank, and they will tell you. Either they know, or they'll dump the contents out of it and start counting.

That's where we're going to start. We're going to count what's in your piggy bank. To help you record everything, we've included a personal balance sheet in the Move into Action section at the end of this chapter. You may want to refer to this tool as you're tallying the contents of your piggy bank.

Step one is to open up your piggy bank and list what you have saved. Okay, as adults we likely have a few more things to count. What else makes up your financial assets, those things you own? Do you own a car or maybe a home? What about all your personal stuff—the contents of your home, your apartment, or wherever you live? Continue to make a list of the major categories and put an estimated value to each item. No need to list every little thing; grouping and summarizing is fine.

Most young children have a piggy bank and very little financial stress. Why so little financial stress? They don't owe anything. We don't extend credit to five-years-olds. No credit means they don't have any liabilities. This being the case, there really isn't much to stress about. Want to go back to that situation and be a kid again? It sounds pretty good, doesn't it? As adults in a credit-driven world, you most likely owe others. You have liabilities that must be accounted for. Common liabilities are your credit card balances, student loans, car loans, and potentially a mortgage on your home. Anything you owe to someone else is a liability and goes onto the list.

So far you've built a list of your assets with associated values, as well as a list of your liabilities with the amounts that you owe. Now, do the following:

1. Total up all the values on the asset list.
2. Total up all the amounts you owe on the liability list.
3. Subtract the total amount of the liabilities from the total amount of your assets, and you have now calculated your financial net worth.

Your net worth might be positive, meaning you have more assets than liabilities, or it might be a negative number, meaning you owe more to others than you own. You've just taken an important step in being a better financial leader. You've created a comprehensive picture of your financial resources. Great leaders always know what resources they have to work with.

Young children grasp a second important financial concept, that of income. Give a kid some money, and his or her thoughts turn to how much to put into the piggy bank and how much to spend. As adults, not too much has changed, has it? Every time you receive your paycheck, the same thought process happens— how much to spend versus how much to save. But life has gotten a lot more complicated than it was when you were a child. You have bills to pay. There is the rent or mortgage payment, car payment, phone bill, cable bill, electric bill, grocery bill, and all the other expenses required just for basic living.

> *A budget is telling your money where to go*
> *instead of wondering where it went.*
> *—Dave Ramsey*

If you haven't guessed the next step already, here it is: you're going to build a budget. We've also included a budget template in the Move into Action section at the end of the chapter. You may want to refer to it as you go through this next exercise. You're going to make two more lists. The first list will include all your income on a monthly basis. This is the amount of your paycheck or perhaps paychecks, as well as any other sources of income. Don't forget to include investment income, though it might vary greatly month to month. Use an annual estimation divided by twelve.

Now create a second list containing all your expenses. Some will be regular expenses that are easy to determine—your rent or mortgage bill, for example, is likely the same each month, as is your car payment. Now think about all the other expenses that might not be monthly. Perhaps you take a vacation or two over the course of the year. Don't forget about things like gifts;

maybe greatest around Christmas, they can really add up. There are many similar expenses that we might call discretionary. If you have more income than expense, you might buy a couple of extra pairs of shoes that you want but technically don't need. Perhaps you treat yourself to dinner at an expensive restaurant. Capture all the ways you spend money on this list.

To complete this exercise, total up your monthly income. Next, total up your monthly expenses. Subtract your expenses from your income. What do you have left? If the number is positive, you have more income than expenses, and some money can go into your piggy bank. If the net result is a negative number, you're outspending your income and you are likely in need of a change in your financial situation. Your piggy bank will become empty very quickly.

▬ The Price of Opportunity

The piggy bank is broken open, and you're determined to go to the candy store. The decision has been made, and the money will be spent. Put yourself in that place and think back to when you literally were a kid in a candy store. As you made your way there, your anticipation was growing. You burst through the doors and looked in awe at all the colors and all the delicious flavors. There were so many choices, and they all looked so good. The adult you were with probably tried to show you different options, usually with the caution that you only had so much to spend. There was so much, though, and you wanted it all! The time ticked down and a choice had to be made. No amount of cajoling would get the adult to give you more. As you handed the clerk your candy and money, the deed was done. There was no going back.

But wait! As you walked down the street, you saw the toy store, the comic book shop, and—*gasp!*—the ice cream stand. The adult was unmoved. Those opportunities had passed you by because you had your mind set on candy. Did you try to force the issue and tell the adult you would give up your next week's allowance or you would do more chores? If you did, it probably didn't work. You clutched your candy bag and walked by all those other choices. In the end, was the candy worth the price you paid?

The lesson to be learned is that the opportunities to buy something were always there, you were just so narrowly focused that you didn't see them. More importantly, you didn't think about what you would be missing out on, even though the adult might have tried to warn you. A candy bar, a small toy, a comic book, or an ice cream cone are small stakes, and the cost of picking one over the other is minimal. After all, they all bring some level of enjoyment, and there is always next time. What happens when the choices aren't so small or the stakes are much higher? Where do you stand if your financial life element is built on a shaky foundation?

There are costs to any choices you make or don't make—opportunity costs—and to increase your personal financial leadership, you must be aware of the impact they have on your ideal future. Decisions about your home, car, activities, or anything else that comprises your lifestyle have to be made with consideration toward what you may be sacrificing in making those choices.

For example, perhaps you have your mind absolutely set on living in a very trendy, urban area, even though the space is small and the rent is very, very high. This is where you want to be, and no one can change your mind. Once you move there, you realize just how small the space is and that there isn't room for all of your things. You have to make arrangements for additional storage—at a price, of course. On top of that, you have to spend even more money to rent a parking space for your car. The costs add up. The worst part is that you wanted to be there because of all the trendy shops and restaurants, but now you can't afford them because you spent all your money on rent, additional storage, and parking. The opportunity costs of living there have taken their toll on the rest of your budget.

This is where you must employ your personal leadership and take ownership of the decisions you made and what you have left behind. Just as you were not forced to choose the candy bar, you were not forced to choose the apartment. Own the decisions you make and do the best you can with them. You might choose the apartment anyway and earn extra money by working in your favorite café, or you might decide to move. Achieving a balance between what is obtained and what the true cost is grows our awareness, which in turn helps us understand the opportunity costs of obtaining our ideal future. Even as adults, we cannot have it all.

Needs versus Wants

Let's get back to the candy store and imagine that you did have the opportunity to buy all you wanted. You bought lots of different candy, gum, new toys, a few comic books, soda, and a huge ice cream sundae. Then you sat down to eat and drink it all. How could it get much better? You had everything you wanted all at once! Yet afterward, the feeling probably wasn't so good. The sick feeling in your stomach started, and life went downhill from there. You didn't even want to play with the toys or read the comics. Having it all was supposed to be the best thing ever, but it really wasn't all that it was cracked up to be. In the end, maybe you would have been far happier with a little candy, a small ice cream, and one toy to play with later. It's one of those valuable lessons we learn when we are young, yet one we so often forget as adults.

What's wrong with wanting it all? Perhaps nothing, as long as we maintain a healthy perspective that it takes time to achieve all of our goals. The real issue surfaces when we become unhappy when we don't get all we want right away. We become confused over the priority of our needs and wants. A need is something that is a basic essential to life. We all need food, shelter, clothing, and the like. Not having one or more of these basic needs is a legitimate source of stress and unhappiness. The confusion starts over things like having the latest cell phone, or newest car, or even grandest vacation. These aren't needs. They are wants, and usually we want them because someone else has them. That isn't the way to build a strong financial life element. To be the personal leader of our own financial situation, we must have absolute clarity about our needs and wants, and how to prioritize them.

All too often, we see people make a critical mistake when they choose to satisfy a want and neglect a need. A great example of this confusion can be seen when people buy the latest cell phone but cannot afford to pay their utility bill. Has this happened to you or someone you know? Societal pressures make having the latest, greatest, coolest cell phone feel very much like a need. Take a step back and really think about it, though. What is really more important—the phone or the heat and electricity in your home? The answer seems obvious. Yet this decision to satisfy wants and neglect needs is repeated over and over. This type of confused decision-making is detrimental to your ideal future because you cannot get there without meeting your basic needs first. Once your needs are met, then and only then can you start fulfilling your wants.

The stress and unhappiness of not having it all is a self-imposed roadblock. You are not a victim because you cannot have all the candy or the cell phone or anything else that is truly just a want. People victimize themselves by making the wrong choices. It is totally on them and you if you fall into this habit. It is your own self-created roadblock. Get over it. Accept it and move on. If you have all your basic needs met, then you aren't a victim. Choose to be a personal leader. Know all the elements in your financial picture; accept what you can have now and what needs to wait a while.

Later on, in chapter 12, we will take this financial knowledge and turn it into financial management through the change-agent factor. Balancing your equation means that you have to have both the life element knowledge you learned here and the change-agent skills we will learn later. It is imperative that you take these separate areas of your equation and bring them together so you can take the action needed to reach your ideal future.

▩ Move into Action: Personal Financial Tools

Use this personal budget template to determine your cash flow—how much money you have coming in (income) versus how much money you have going out (expenses)—and the amount of surplus income that can be directed toward savings. If expenses are greater than income, you are likely off track from obtaining your ideal future. Refer back to the "Your Piggy Bank" section above for more directions.

Personal Balance Sheet

Assets (What You Own)		Approximate Value
Current Assets		
Cash (checking account balance)		
Savings account		
Money market		
Certificates of deposit		
Other liquid cash assets		
Total Current Assets		
Investments		
Stocks		
Bonds		
Mutual funds		
IRA		
401K		
Annuity		
Life insurance cash value		
Other financial investments		
Total Investments		
Personal Assets		
Furniture		
Vehicles (car, boat, motorcycle, etc.)		
Primary home		
Other property (camp, land, rental property)		
Art, jewelry, other collectibles		
Other		
Total Personal Assets		
Total Assets		

Liabilities (What You Owe)		Approximate Value
Current Liabilities (payment due within twelve months)		
Credit cards		
Other short-term debts		
Total Current Liabilities		
Medium- and Long-Term Liabilities		
Car loans		
Personal loans		
Mortgage		
Home equity loans		
Other mortgages		
Student loans		
Other loans		
Total Medium- and Long-Term Liabilities		
Total Liabilities		
Recap		
Total Assets		
Total Liabilities		
Net Worth		

Personal Budget Template

	Monthly Amount	Yearly Total
Income		
Monthly take-home pay (after taxes, health insurance, and retirement contributions)		
Other monthly income (if applicable)		
Annual bonus income (if applicable)		
Monetary gifts (birthdays, holidays, etc.)		
Other cash receipts (tax refunds, credit rewards, rebates)		
Total Income		
Living Expenses (Basic Needs)		
Housing (rent or mortgage, including taxes)		
Utilities (water and gas/electric, as applicable)		
Grocery and household-supply expenses		
Car expense (payment, upkeep) or transportation costs		
Insurance (homeowners, renters, or car as applicable)		
Health costs (insurance copays, prescriptions)		
Phone bill		
Clothing allowance		
Other loan payments (credit cards, student loans, personal loans, and so on)		
Child care (if applicable)		

Subtotal Living Expenses		
Other Expenses		
Cable/Internet/streaming services bills		
Donations		
Entertainment		
Gifts (birthdays, holidays, weddings, and so on) *Tip: total for the year and divide by twelve months*		
Home improvement and repair funds		
Pet costs		
Other miscellaneous expenses		
Subtotal Other Expenses		
Pay Yourself First: Savings		
Monthly savings		
Additional retirement savings		
Life insurance, long-term care insurance, and other similar expenses		
Subtotal Savings Expenses		
BUDGET TOTALS **(Total income minus all expenses)**		

CHAPTER 5

Your Career

Most people don't think of their career as a launchpad, but it is the final piece of the life element factor. After all, unless you're independently wealthy, you need to work for the income. The idea, though, is to look beyond the paycheck. You spend a good portion of your adult life and waking hours at work. Your career has an economic, social, emotional, mental, and even physical impact on your world. If you aren't on the right trajectory at work, it becomes nearly impossible to be on the path to your ideal future.

Your ideal future should be a lofty destination, and the journey there should be filled with happiness, joy, and pride. Now think of your career: What do you feel? Have you aimed high? Are you enjoying the benefits of reaching those heights, or are you are going nowhere because you're in an endless cycle of being unfulfilled, unhappy, and uninspired?

Those who view their career as a launchpad are harnessing the incredible power of forward progress. They are reaching their heights because they know their mind-set is the fuel they need to break through outside forces. Just as rockets have to overcome the powerful force of gravity, we have to do the same with anything that stands between us and our ideal future. It doesn't take high technology and huge rockets to accomplish this; all we need is the right attitude and mind-set.

Becoming a personal leader allows you to take ownership, chart your own course, and accept the challenges that lie ahead. In a sense, you become the commander on this launchpad, and you will need to understand your role and the tools you need to maximize the leverage from your launch.

> *Don't make career choices on short-term financial gain.*
> *Job satisfaction and career enjoyment are far more important.*
> —*Henry Samueli, PhD*

■ You're the Commander

One of the key aspects of any leadership role is the need to assess. Whether it is your team, the available resources, or the tasks that need to be completed, the commander must always gauge what is required to get to the end result. It is imperative that you fully understand whether your current job is a lifelong career that brings fulfillment or simply a way to make ends meet. Just as the commander assesses the current situation and at the same time adjusts the course as needed, we too must monitor and adjust as we move toward our ideal future.

Regardless of how you feel about going to work, there is a key assessment that must be faced. It is one of the toughest questions to answer. Here it is: Do I see a path forward from my job today that ends at my desired destination, my ideal future? To help you answer this question, you have to think about where you want to be in your career, where you realistically think you'll be, and how it leads to obtaining all the items that comprise your ideal future.

Start thinking about your career five years from now and keep going from there. What are your takeaways? Even though you love your job, the realization might be that there is limited growth potential. While you love it now, ultimately the end result may be frustration. In other situations, the work you may be doing now is not what you want to do forever, yet it is a stepping-stone that must be crossed along the way. In doing this assessment, you're the commander who must decide whether to continue on the current course or abort the mission.

You might like the company, your coworkers, and your customers, but liking them won't matter if it doesn't ultimately bring you to your desired end result. It is truly your decision. You absolutely cannot delegate control to someone else because it removes you from commanding your future, and then you're merely going along for the ride. Leadership by definition means you are commanding your future. If you choose to just go along for the ride, you're following someone else. You've handed your ideal future to another person. Why would you ever do this?

▓▓ Gauges and Instruments

You'll need to look at various factors to execute this part of the equation. Just as a commander uses the information from gauges and instruments, so must you. We have provided you the gauges to comprise your instrument panel. Each one correlates to an aspect of your career. To help you with this process, you will find a summary of all the gauges in the Move into Action section at the end of this chapter, with boxes to guide you through assessing your own levels.

Instrument #1: Financial Benefits

People work to earn an income to sustain their life and hopefully grow their future. In choosing an employer, there is a reasonable expectation to be paid close to the position's worth. Unfortunately, all too often, that is an assumption people make rather than a fact they know. Additionally, it is the total financial benefit package that needs to be assessed rather than salary alone. Compensation comes in many forms, including vacation time, sick time, various forms of insurance, retirement plan contributions, paid training, and many other potential components. All told, these nonsalary financial benefits commonly comprise between 20 and 40 percent of total compensation. Therefore, it is essential to consider the financial benefit package in its totality.

By researching and formulating your market value based on all of these benefits, you will be able to accurately assess this component of your life element. For example, if similar positions in your area, with similar experience and education, earn an average of $50,000, then that is what your expectation of market value should be. If you then compare it to your current salary of $35,000, your financial benefit meter is reading about 70 percent. Whether this is or isn't acceptable will be determined when you look at the whole instrument panel. The key point is to have an accurate reading on this gauge so the correct decisions can be made.

Fortunately, the task of researching what your market value is has become a lot easier. There is a great deal of information available to you. There are now websites dedicated to salary information: try www.payscale.com and www.salary.com. Many professional industry groups publish salary information that you may be able to access. Various government entities also conduct salary surveys and publish this information; see what's available right at your local library. Lastly, talk to employment agencies and recruiters in your area. They are likely to have a good grasp on what similar positions in your area are paying.

Piloting Your Career Tip
Never, ever ask your coworkers about their salary. This is personal information that should not be shared. Keep your salary confidential and allow others to do the same.

Instrument #2: Life Balance

Understanding the balance between the needs of your personal and work life is essential. As much as we might try, issues and situations in our personal life do carry over into our daily jobs. We can avoid admitting it as much as possible, we might even think we are successfully hiding it, but it is still there. By creating a life balance meter, we can honestly look at how we may or may not be fulfilling the requirements of both aspects of our lives.

For example, let's assume your current job offers flexible scheduling. This is a tremendous benefit to you because you can safely put your kids on the bus in the morning. The meter is ticking higher for better balance. If it is the reverse, though, and you're in a position that is very regimented, it becomes a struggle to meet your personal needs. The meter ticks lower toward a lack of balance.

Whether it is your kids, pets, parents, or anything else that is personally important to you, it has to be assessed within this meter. Consider your needs versus the employer's requirements in areas like flexibility of work hours, expectation to work overtime or extended hours, sick- and vacation-time policies, amount of travel required, and benefits that might be very valuable to you, like on-site day care. In the life-balance box, list your personal needs and your employer's requirements, and see how they match up. Use this tool to judge your position and as one of the instruments for charting the course of your career.

Instrument #3: Cultural Fit

In chapter 2, you listed your values and ethics. They are a core life element. In this section, we take it one step further to determine how well they match those of your employer. These values create a culture within an organization, and by developing a cultural fit instrument, you can gauge whether you're in conflict or in harmony with this culture.

While you're at work, you must uphold the values of your employer. It doesn't matter whether you agree with them or not; by agreeing to work for your employer, you're agreeing to act within that culture. You're being paid to complete the tasks assigned to you and in the manner expected. As a salesperson, you may be working in an organization that encourages the sale at any cost. The manager tells you to do whatever it takes, potentially to the point of being dishonest, just get the deal signed. If honesty is one of your values, then by using this instrument, you will clearly see the reading as a negative measurement. You're in conflict every time you are forcing a sale to go through. Obviously, being in conflict leads nowhere fast. It makes it nearly impossible to reach your ideal future. You would be far better off in a culture that wants the customer to make the most informed decision possible.

The cultural fit gauge is your chance to look at the similarities and differences you have with your current employer. List them within the cultural fit box and determine if the meter is positive or negative.

• According to human resources expert Susan M. Heathfield, "Culture is made up of the values, beliefs, underlying assumptions, attitudes, and behaviors shared by a group of people. Culture is the behavior that results when a group arrives at a set of—generally unspoken and unwritten—rules for working together."

Instrument #4: Growth Dial

The growth dial indicates whether you're in a position that has the potential to grow into the next milestone or not. If you find yourself at a dead end with no opportunity to advance within your organization, the needle points to zero. If there is an abundance of opportunity to move forward and move closer to meeting your full potential, then the dial reads closer to 100 percent.

In the growth-dial box, realistically determine what your next position should be, your time frame for reaching it, and whether it is obtainable within your current organization. By doing so, you will have a simple yet important instrument to gauge your progress toward obtaining your ideal future.

Instrument #5: Learning Spectrum

Once again, this is an instrument that ties back to an earlier chapter—chapter 3 on education and lifelong learning. To have a solid foundation, a launchpad, you have to have the education elements you need to advance. There is a spectrum of support which has a low end and a high end of time and money offered to further your learning. If you're working for a company that encourages its employees to achieve certain certifications or attend conferences, the gauge would read high for this instrument. The company is willing to make an investment in you, and that investment will help you on your way to your ideal future. The gauge reads low when the company offers little or no investment toward your development.

Roe and Don Polczynski Jr.

In the learning-spectrum box, list all the education initiatives you want or need for your career development. Then list how your employer either helps or hinders the process. Comparing the two will define where the needle points in your education spectrum.

Instrument #6: Scope of Fulfillment

On one end of the fulfillment scope is dread, but at the opposite end is passion. Think about a schoolteacher whose passion was to facilitate learning in young students. The teacher then transferred to an administrative position that both paid more and had more career growth opportunity. The teacher, no longer in a classroom filled with young minds excited to learn, found the new administrative position completely unfulfilling, to the point where she dreaded the drive to school each morning. In this situation, the teacher began on the high end of the scope with a passion for teaching and transferred to a position where the passion was no longer being fulfilled, ultimately resulting in the loss of this positive energy ending in dread.

Where does your scope align? List all the things in your job that you find fulfilling. Now list everything you dread. Compare the two lists. Determine your position on the scope of fulfillment.

Deploying the Instrument Panel

As you review all of these instruments, remember that each one presents a part of the picture for this factor. No one dial tells the whole story. The final action is to place your own level of importance on each dial, as they do vary greatly from person to person. Taking all the dials into account, you will be able to determine if your current career path can help you to reach your dreams or what changes need to be made to get there.

54

This isn't a one-and-done usage, either. You can use the instrument panel in this chapter at any time to monitor and adjust as your life's journey unfolds. By completing these tasks, you are truly being the personal leader, even commander, you need to be to obtain your ideal future.

▓▓ Move into Action: The Career Instrument Panel

This exercise will guide you to a better understanding of how you can personally use the six elements of your career as a launchpad. Use these gauges and their summary notes as a starting point to create your own instrument panel. Create a spreadsheet with a tab for each dial and corresponding box or just use a notebook— whatever works best for you. Conduct your research and track your progress for each gauge. As you develop the information, the path to your ideal future will be clearer.

Financial Benefits	Life Balance	Cultural Fit	Growth Dial	Learning Spectrum	Scope of Fulfillment
Determine the percentage of your current salary compared to the local average.	What do you need to maintain a career/life balance?	Compare your values and ethics list to your employer's culture.	Realistically determine what your next position should be.	List all of the education initiatives you want or need for your career development.	List all the things in your job you find fulfilling.
Add in all the other benefits you receive, such as insurances, time off, and retirement contributions.	How do your current employer's policies align with your needs?	How much are you in alignment with your employer's culture?	What is the time frame to reach it?	List how your employer helps or hinders the process.	List all that you dread on your drive to work.
Do you find this amount to be acceptable when looking at the whole instrument panel?	Is there a balance that is easily maintained?	Is the difference acceptable to you?	Is it obtainable within your current organization?	Compare the results. Where are the gaps?	Which side outweighs the other?

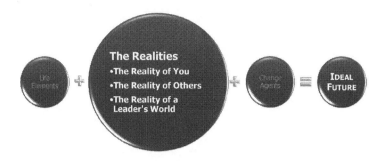

Section 2
THE REALITIES

There is so much to filter through that it can be a challenge to determine what is real based upon fact and what is not. Our perceptions of reality can become twisted by so many outside influences that we lose sight of just how negative their impact can be. We may not be portraying a true image of our inner self and instead focusing too much on what we think the world wants to see. The people who surround us may not be as engaged with us as we think.

When we get past the surface on these levels, we begin to understand the realities that are ever present in our lives. The truth is there for us to use as a way to find the actual answers to the questions. Once we accept what is real, we will be able to understand the realities of our ideal future. This factor examines three main dimensions to understanding this reality: the reality of you, the reality of others, and the reality of a leader's world.

Face reality as it is, not as it was or you wish it to be.
—Jack Welch

CHAPTER 6

The Reality of You

Think about a recent phenomenon that has taken hold not only in our country but also in many parts of the world. It is something that has spread across people of all ages, economic backgrounds, and cultures. There are even products that have been introduced as a direct result of this movement. If you haven't guessed yet, we are talking about the selfie. From presidents to celebrities, from the Pope to average people, it has become commonplace to turn the camera toward oneself. It goes beyond just taking the picture—selfies are then shared across many outlets. It has become a new form of communication with its own applications, such as Snapchat, to encourage the use of self-images.

When people post a selfie, they are posting an image they are trying to portray. Oftentimes it is a reflection of how they have been influenced by the media and the entertainment world. They are trying to give the audience a view of how they fit the cultural norm. In the end, however, it is just an image, and probably doesn't reflect true reality. In posing for the perfect shot, what they are really doing is hiding the twenty other pictures they took while trying to get the perfect one. In looking at the reality of you, we have to view all of those pictures. The real you is the picture of you with your eyes closed or hair that isn't strategically placed. To determine what your ideal future should be, you have to determine who you are and what is even realistically possible.

In discovering "The Reality of You," you're looking past your image into your strengths and weaknesses, your abilities and restrictions, your talents and natural gifts. After this introspection, the real picture of you needs to be turned into a panoramic view of your place in the world that surrounds you. When you have achieved the balance of the inner and outer views, then you will know the reality of achieving your ideal future.

> *The camera makes everyone a tourist in*
> *other people's reality, and eventually their own.*
> —*Susan Sontag*

▩ Taking Your Inner Selfie

Suppose for a moment that we set aside all those traditional selfies and spent some time viewing ourselves from a new perspective. This new perspective is one of inner reflection—getting to know our various dimensions from the inside out. When we don't understand ourselves as we are today, we cannot define what our future can and should be.

How do you even get started with developing the picture of inner reflection? It starts with uncovering the dimensions that comprise who you are. There may be a lot to learn and discover on the inside that you have never really considered. After all, you've probably looked into a mirror most days of your life. Now you're going to look into a new kind of mirror and see a different type of picture.

Some of these dimensions have already been covered in the life elements section and include relationships, values and ethics, education, finances, and career. The knowledge you have gained from the foundations that have been built are at your core and comprise part of your inner self. In building the reality of you, we are expanding on that foundation to the next dimensions of personality, natural tendencies, talents, and interests. While this might not be a totally inclusive list, these four dimensions will give you a good start on this new perspective.

Personality
- According to Dictionary.com, personality can be defined as "a person as an embodiment of a collection of qualities."

Personality

Personality is a primary aspect of the reality we live in. We are who we are, which makes it important to have a clear understanding of personality as a dimension. Let's consider the common situation of making a career selection. Suppose you're considering a career in sales that will involve creating a network of people and building relationships with them. Do you consider yourself an introvert or an extrovert? Do you actually know, or are you making an assumption about yourself? If you're introverted, you probably dread the thought of networking dinners where you'll spend hours trying to make small talk with strangers. The extroverts reading this, on the other hand, are likely thinking of this as an energizing and enjoyable activity. Knowing that you're an introvert doesn't mean you can't have a great sales career, but it suggests that you may not find some aspects of it to be enjoyable.

To gain this level of understanding and to ascertain to what degree you have these personality traits, the first step is to take a personality assessment or two. Such assessments have been around for a very long time and were an early method of taking an inner selfie. What's changed since then is the amount of science behind them and their availability, accessibility, and affordability via the Internet. Their use has exploded, and they now should be among the methods you utilize to take an inner selfie.

Two assessments you can get started with are the Myers-Briggs and the DiSC profiles. These are available via the Internet at low cost and have a substantial amount of research behind them. You may learn more about them and purchase them at www.mbtionline.com and www.discprofile.com, respectively. You may have already encountered these assessments, as many employers utilize them. If you cannot access your previous results, take them again. The best part in taking any of these profile assessments is the interpretation the companies provide upon completion. The summary reports provide a picture of your personality dimension.

Talents

- According to Dictionary.com, talent can be defined as both "a special natural ability or aptitude" and "a capacity for achievement or success."

Talents

The next dimension to examine is that of your talents. You possess certain strengths and tendencies that occur naturally to form your talents. They aren't learned, they are just a part of who you are. There are assessments that will help you gain clarity on these abilities. Once you have gained this understanding, you can apply these natural strengths and tendencies to propel you toward your ideal future.

Two of our favorite tools for assessing talents are the Kolbe A Index profile and *StrengthsFinder 2.0*. The Kolbe A Index is a great tool that will help you understand some of your natural tendencies and talents, such as the likelihood you'll complete what you start or an innate ability to make quick decisions. Surprisingly, many of our talents are instinctual. These may be referred to as our "mode of operation." We are actually born with these instincts. Understanding what is instinctual to you will allow you to harness more of these talents. Making the most of your natural talents is an important part of your inner selfie.

The Kolbe A Index is available directly from Kolbe at www .kolbe.com. After taking this assessment, you will better understand how you naturally react to situations. You'll also learn why it may be easy to work with others with similar profiles and why you may be in conflict with those having opposing profiles. With this knowledge, your inner selfie will come into much greater focus.

StrengthsFinder 2.0 by Tom Rath[1] is a very popular book that contains a code for an online assessment. The research and science behind *StrengthsFinder* concludes that we all act in accordance with thirty-four themes of talent. The assessment results will show which five talent themes are strongest within you and how you can apply them to your benefit. Focusing on making the most of your talents is a good way to maximize your potential. Trying to strengthen your weaknesses is generally a losing strategy that will result in a large waste of energy and ultimately frustration. Working in harmony with your natural talents is the path of least resistance and will lead you to greater accomplishments and joy.

> **Reality of You Tip**
>
> When you receive the results from your inner-selfie assessments, don't focus on the weaknesses. Your attention should go toward your strengths and how you can capitalize on them to reach your ideal future.

In thinking about the talent dimension, we all inherently have a sense of what we are good at, and it's probably the same things that we enjoy doing. When we capitalize on these skills and talents, we are using them to reach our ideal future. Surprisingly, we are not aware of some of them, or we misdirect ourselves to what we think we should be good at instead.

To get a different view of your abilities, simply ask others who know you—whether they be coworkers, friends, or family members—what they see as your true talents. You might be surprised and enlightened by what others see in you. Compare these results to your own thoughts and efforts, and remember that it may be time to redirect efforts if a skill just isn't a strong one for you. Whatever your skills and talents are, they must be captured as part of your inner selfie so you can maximize them in your progress toward personal leadership and your ideal future.

Interests

The final dimension we are going to highlight is your interests. This layer of your inner selfie is probably the most pronounced. If someone were to ask you what your hobbies are or what you like to do, the answers will usually come naturally. That doesn't mean, though, that you shouldn't actively manage them. Capturing the positive energy you get from these pursuits will motivate you to push forward. It will also help you to determine where the future could go.

Your interests are the things that will bring joy and meaning to your ideal future. Perhaps you have interests that you can't pursue at the moment. That's okay. Capture them now, and you'll be better prepared to take advantage of opportunities when they show up at your door. Too often people reach retirement after working hard all their adult years, only to have no idea what to do with their lives. How can this be? In the midst of their daily toil, little or no time was dedicated to considering what their true interests were or what would deliver joy and meaning in their golden years. Unfortunately, because of this simple omission, retirement becomes an unfulfilling stretch of life instead of one filled with joy and meaning fit for an ideal future.

Once you consider all these dimensions, the traditional selfie may seem to be paper thin. That's because it is; it lacks depth. An outward selfie is just that—a two-dimensional representation that shows a very limited and incomplete picture. As a personal leader, you'll find that relying on traditional images will not suffice.

▓▓ The Panoramic View

Now that the true picture of your inner reality has been revealed, the focus needs to shift outward, toward a panoramic view of the world. Each of us has a place, and there are boundaries around us. Some are frontiers that allow us to blaze new trails, while others are borders that keep us contained. As much as we may not want to admit it, there is a limit to what is achievable. Knowing how you and your ideal future fit into the world that surrounds you is key to bringing everything into sharp focus. To do so, you need to take your newly discovered knowledge of your personality, natural tendencies, talents, and interests and realistically determine how far the frontiers can be pushed and where the true boundaries lie.

Over the course of your life, new frontiers will become available and new boundaries will be set. The world will change; in fact, it will change faster and faster. You will change, sort of. Yes, your selfies will look different. Perhaps your hair will turn gray or you will have less of it. Some wrinkles will find their way into the picture. Your basic personality and many of your innate tendencies will likely stand the test of time, however. Understanding the real you is a tremendous advantage in the face of all this other change.

Have you ever met a travel agent? There used to be one in every neighborhood shopping center, helping people with airline tickets, hotel reservations, and other travel-related activities. It was a popular career choice for people who were outgoing, sales-oriented, and great at planning details. Yet with the advent of the Internet, the travel-agency industry grew very weak and is fading more and more with time. While you might have the qualities that were once sought after by travel agencies, it is now a border that isn't worth attempting to cross. The reality is that the industry changed dramatically, eliminating the need for human travel agents, who have been replaced by travel websites. This is a reality that is unlikely to change; it's a boundary. That's okay, you need to adapt to a new frontier.

Being a great planner means that you are probably great at follow-through, and with that and a love for travel, there are other options to pursue. These might include writing travel blogs or leading tour groups. Look for opportunities that combine your multiple dimensions with the reality of a panoramic view. It doesn't matter what they are, as the key is to take your personality, tendencies, talents, and interests and apply them to the world around you. By doing so, you will be developing your complete selfie.

Choices, almost infinite in number, face us throughout our lifetime. The choice of what comprises our ideal future is up to each of us. Likewise are the number of paths we can choose in our lifetime. Some of the available paths do lead to our ideal future, while others lead us far from it. Use your newfound knowledge of your inner selfie to discover which paths are more realistic than others. The fact that one path is best for your friend is in no way an indication that it will be the correct one for you. Remember—you're leading your own way, not following someone else's. Take every opportunity to continue to learn and refine your picture of yourself.

CHAPTER 7

The Reality of Others

It's time to turn the camera around from selfie view to look at the reality of others. It can take a great deal of time to nurture relationships to the point where the real person comes through. Success in life is built on relationships, and it is important that we try to know others as much as we try to know ourselves.

Consider this: You are a sitting at a large conference table with your peers, your friends, even your family. It doesn't matter who is there, as long as they play a part in your world. As you're sitting there, an outsider comes in and puts a colorfully wrapped package in the center of the table. Everyone starts to wonder what is inside. One person might think it is a set of keys for a car he desperately needs. Someone else imagines it to be the diamond engagement ring she has waited so long for. The group all starts to talk about how sure they are it is something they want or need. Even you join in and begin to consider all the possibilities that are close to your heart. Heated discussions might even ensue as all assembled want that package to be for them.

People become convinced that the gift contains their want or wish, and they have little regard for the reality of others. It can even get to the point where hostility takes hold and feelings are hurt. But here's the secret: until the wrappings come off, everyone

67

is right. We are all allowed to have our personal opinions. Real leaders accept this and help the group see that all viewpoints are valid. When we reverse the selfie and look at others, we see their value as unique individuals.

In your world, do you view yourself as unique? Are you convinced there is no one else in the world exactly like you? Now look around: Do you see that same uniqueness in each and every person? Or have you already started to lump people into groups? Perhaps you're looking at a group of college students all around the age of twenty and immediately classify them with all the general characteristics of millennials. You don't know them, yet you convince yourself that they are all alike. How easy it is to group people together and assume they are all the same.

Where did the uniqueness go? Somehow we replaced uniqueness with sameness. It just makes understanding the world easier. Therein lies the problem. Trying to make those around you easy to understand is unrealistic; the true reality of others is lost in the process.

When the uniqueness of those around us is lost, the personal is transformed into the impersonal. Instead of seeing each person as uniquely different, we apply preconceived notions. With our inflexible viewpoints in place, the need to understand each individual is lost. When we make things personal, we can understand each person's realities. We touch those around us individually, and all will remember uniquely and differently how we made them feel.

Making It Personal

Leadership is personal and intimate, and many people are confused about the difference between deep, personally intimate relationships and mere acquaintanceships. A personal, intimate relationship is one in which you can be completely candid and vulnerable while simultaneously generous and accountable to the other person. We think we know a lot about the people who surround us, but we don't take the time to make the actual connections personal. Nor do we allow them to see the personal side of ourselves. It leaves the relationship lacking, because we are losing the ability to learn from each other's reality. There are multiple sides to every story, and we are growing more and more accustomed to just caring about the highlights.

Social media has influenced how we view the people around us. Because we are exposed to a person's tweets or texts or posts, it's easy to think we understand the person. After all, how can it be any clearer? It is all there in black and white. Now imagine those same words coming from a person standing across from you. What would you hear? What would you interpret?

Most of the physical aspects of communication are unconsciously read. As you first hear the words, you may or may not notice their particular volume. Maybe the person is speaking loudly, maybe very softly. The words have a tone. Perhaps the words are expressed tersely or with great caring. Beyond the audible, your mind would interpret the visual. What do you see and understand when you look into the eyes of another person— fear, rage, tears of sadness, tears of joy? Next, notice the person's hands, and whether the gestures match the words spoken. Take note of the person's posture and any other movements. Notice if the person perhaps is trembling.

Just as you're absorbing all of this person's physical and verbal cues, he or she is reading the same from you. Interest level, empathy, advice, and more are among the cues you are unconsciously giving back. Face-to-face communication brings the conversation alive. Now how personal does that post, text, or tweet really seem? It seems a lot less personal than it did a moment ago. The reality of others cannot be captured in mere words. It must be captured in all its various dimensions.

Capturing these dimensions means you're making it personal. You're becoming aware of the reality of others. You're respecting their differences. Not only that, but you're allowing them to see the reality of who you are as well.

Though social media can be superficial, it can also be a great start to developing relationships, as long as you keep in mind its limitations. It is nice to catch up with old friends and get to know new ones. It can't just stop there, though. For relationships to be valuable, they have to be intimate and personal. You must allow the relationships to develop further.

One great way is to share experiences—perhaps a dinner out, a game night, or even a camping trip. It doesn't matter much what you are doing as long as it increases the level of engagement. When we come together is when we truly get to experience the uniqueness of others. Allow yourself to learn about them and from them. It is this open learning process that will give you the knowledge you need to become a personal leader and obtain your ideal future.

Reality of Others Tip

Make a point of saying good morning and good night to the people you work closely with. It is a powerful connecting point that should not be underestimated. Through these small acts of engagement, we can see more of others' realities. The connections will become stronger on all sides, and it is a good daily reminder to them about how much you care.

Understanding the Other Person's Reality

Once the door is open in a relationship, the next step is to begin to understand the other person's reality. As we go through life, we have good days and bad days. There are pressures from careers, family, friends, and even the world. This is the uniqueness factor again. Everyone has different triggers and needs. We can build better relationships if we just take the time to understand someone else's point of view.

If someone acts out, instead of trying to delve deeper into what is really going on, often people will just say, "What is his problem?" The problem is a lack of understanding. Why don't we just ask the person why he or she feels that way? An answer may lead you down a particular path and to another question, and before you know it you have developed an understanding of someone's reality at far deeper level.

Speak less. Ask more. Listen carefully. A mind-set of seeking to understand others is the foundation for uncovering their true reality. If we want others to understand us, we should start by trying to understand them.

Seeking to understand does involve time and effort. Sometimes it might even feel like work. In our busy lives, do we really have the energy to get to know others at a deeper level? Think about what happens when we don't bother or just give it a halfhearted try. People know when someone is being genuine with them—or if they don't know at first, they soon find out. Leadership has a natural pull that makes people want to follow and support whatever the cause may be. As personal leaders, we must be genuine in our efforts to get to know others. An increase in closeness, to any degree, opens doors to better relationships.

> *There is a difference between listening and*
> *waiting for your turn to speak.*
> *—Simon Sinek*

■ How You Make Them Feel

Emotional intelligence may be one of the most important attributes of a leader. People are every bit as emotional as they are logical. Failing to understand people's emotions is failing to understand a very large part of who they are and their true reality. If you have any doubt about this, think about a conversation with someone from a year or two ago. Do you remember many details of that conversation? You likely don't. What you almost certainly do remember is how the other person made you feel. If someone is having a bad day, is he or she going to feel better for seeing you, or are you just adding to the burden? Whichever the case, you will be remembered on some level, and it will influence the person's response to your next encounter.

Consider your favorite restaurant. Let's say that the food is great but there is one waitress no one wants to face. She is always negative, always complaining about too much work and not enough recognition. Even the simplest request is met with resistance. Asking for something special means you're entering the danger zone. You know there will be issues. It isn't an enticing prospect, and it is just not worth the bother. Ultimately, as good as the food is, you don't feel like dealing with the hassle.

How will this low emotional intelligence affect the waitress's career and ideal future? More than likely, her attitude and approach will hinder her prospects. Would you want to keep her on your team when she can be so miserable? Probably not. While she might have future dreams and plans, she hasn't made other people feel like she is worth their help. If only she had exercised some emotional intelligence and realized that she needed to make her customers feel valued, she would change her ways and become the waitress everyone asks for.

Clearly, you must now put your emotional intelligence to work. Here's one of the best ways to get started. Before going out to that networking event, party, job interview, or social gathering, ask yourself how you want to make people feel after meeting you. Do you have a project you want to engage them in? Are you looking to increase your sphere of influence? What value can you bring to others? Once you have the answers, you'll be much more in tune with those around you.

Perhaps you will change the way you greet others, shift the conversation to more about them, or ask more engaging questions. Maybe you'll make more eye contact or give a warmer handshake or a hug. Consider throwing in some humor and positivity. Chances are, others will naturally gravitate toward you. You'll connect and see more deeply as you increase your attention on how your words and actions translate into others' emotions. Allow others to see the genuine you, and in return you'll not only see more of others' realities, you'll make emotional connections that will long be remembered.

Before we can go about enacting the change that will move us toward our ideal future, it is absolutely necessary to understand the reality of those around us. Embrace the fact that leadership is personal, very personal. Doing so will reveal so much more detail in the world around you. Add in some emotional intelligence, and you'll see more than just uniqueness—you'll see and feel the world in more dimensions. It may take some time to adjust to this new reality, but that's okay—just don't wait to get started. As a personal leader, it is totally within your ability to reveal the emotional side that may have previously gone unseen. Enjoy the view of this new reality and continue the journey to your ideal future.

The Realities
•The Reality of You
•The Reality of Others
•The Reality of a
Leader's World

Life
Elements

Change
Agents

IDEAL
FUTURE

CHAPTER 8

The Reality of a Leader's World

Chances are, if you watch any programs on television, you're aware of "reality shows." Maybe you watch some of them and perhaps even enjoy them. Many of these shows focus on careers, lifestyles, or family dynamics. Every network seems to have its own version, which it runs over and over. However, if you really look at these shows from a leader's perspective, you know there is nothing *real* about them.

In developing your personal leadership, you need to understand that leaders don't subscribe to the philosophies depicted in the context of a program designed to draw viewers in, with the intent to increase ratings and personal wealth. Your real focus needs to be on finding fulfillment in the development of your own personal ideal future. As personal leaders, we find that our lives and actions are often the exact opposite of what is portrayed in reality television. To live in the world of a leader's reality, we must act by building others up instead of tearing them down. We must avoid acting with vengeance or self-pity; we must act with generosity, not greed.

75

In accepting these conditions, we must also be aware that it is very likely the many people we come into contact with will have their view of reality skewed by what they have been watching day in and day out. For far too many, the unreal world has been adopted as the real world. It is time to put a stop to it. Begin by changing the channel to Leadership TV.

> *If your actions inspire others to dream more, learn more,*
> *do more, and become more, you are a leader.*
> —*John Quincy Adams*

"Attitude is everything" is not a cliché; it's a leader's reality. Fortunately, attitudes are readily available to everyone. Let's look at three that inspire leaders.

Attitude #1: Building Up versus Tearing Down

Leaders elect to make the world a better place by building others up, creating new leaders—so much so that their goal is often to create others greater than themselves. You too must accept this responsibility and the mind-set to grow others. As leadership expert Steve Farber, author of *Greater Than Yourself: The Ultimate Lesson of True Leadership*, writes, "Real leadership ... is an extreme act rooted in love and motivated by a desire to create a better world—whether it's the world of your company, team, neighborhood, or family."[2]

A leader's greatness comes as a direct result of his or her positive impact—who that leader has grown, not torn down. The process isn't as difficult as it seems. You have a lot of material with which to build others up. Share your knowledge, connections, experience, advice, life lessons, confidence, encouragement, candid feedback, and perhaps most important, your time.

So you've got all this to share, and you should just do it and that's it, right? Not quite. Start by learning more about those who are a part of your world. Find out their personal hopes and dreams. Rather than using that knowledge as a weapon against them, use it as a higher power to help them whenever and wherever you can. Shrinking their learning curve will actually expand your own learning opportunities. This act of enabling starts small, but as you develop this new approach, the impact grows bigger and bigger. There are many opportunities to learn more about yourself as you help others in their personal quest for success.

Ultimately, your goal is to create a succession plan of leaders. So often your advancement—at work, within an organization, and in general—is dependent upon having someone to succeed you. The goal is to create a potential successor; by doing so, you have just made yourself promotable. You are building up the team behind you so you can move forward. This value will be fully recognized by increased performance for you, the team, and ultimately the organization.

Realizing the power of switching the channel is immense. It is powerful enough to enable you to make big strides toward your ideal future. Those who believe and act in a manner that grows others, building on what they have and sharing their gifts, grow themselves as a result and are living in a leader's world.

▨ Attitude #2: No Victims Allowed

When you watch a television reality show, you allow the characters to draw you into the drama of their woes and the trauma of their vengeance. It is your choice. You aren't forced to watch it or to believe that it is anything close to the truth. Only through careful scripting and editing does it come across as true.

Apparently vengeance and self-pity are great for television ratings. But they aren't part of the world that leaders live in. Let's be a little clearer on that. Leaders lead; they don't seek revenge on others, and they don't wallow helplessly in self-pity. Since these behaviors are rampant in society, leaders do have to contend with people who choose to play these roles. Remember—just as you shouldn't immerse yourself in the world of reality television, you should also not accept the invitation from those who want to involve you with their dubious behaviors.

When we are surrounded by people who may not act with the best intentions or even maliciously try to cause harm, it can be very easy to want to get even. The need for retribution becomes a way to heal the damage—or so it may seem. We have been injured, hurt, maybe even embarrassed, so we must act. Yet when we do so, no healing occurs. The wounds are still there, and they might even be compounded by new ones added in the latest confrontation. What we fail to recognize is that we were not trying to heal; we were using vengeance as a defense mechanism.

Keeping on the high road is often difficult. The temptation to stoop to the offender's level is very real. Don't do it! As difficult as it may sound, leaders move forward by granting forgiveness, not by exacting revenge.

Self-pity is a self-defeating attitude that ultimately robs you of the momentum you need to move toward your ideal future. That is not to say that leaders are without emotional needs. After all, allowing some vulnerability to show is a tool leaders can use to engage others. When something in life goes wrong—and it does happen—there is nothing wrong with wanting others to show a little empathy or sympathy toward a difficult situation. As long as it stops there, it is fine. But when people take on the attitude and role of a complete victim, they choose to become helpless—powerless to lead their own life. They have abdicated the responsibility to lead.

How can a leader navigate those tough situations when the trap of vengeance and victimhood are so close by? True leaders turn their focus toward finding a better way for everyone involved.

Life offers many invitations to seek revenge or play the role of victim. What sets leaders apart is that they don't accept such roles. Yes, it is just that simple. Say no to vengeance, and don't allow yourself to be helpless with self-pity.

There is a second role for the leader which can be just as important. Good leaders know when to be great followers. A leader will not feel victimized because someone else has the spotlight. A leader will not seek revenge because someone else had a better idea. Leaders will give the spotlight to others and promote their ideas when it is in the best interest of everyone involved. They will set the standard by showing a willingness to follow others. By embracing this mind-set you will continually position yourself to play two keys roles: leader and follower.

Leader's Reality Tip
Count your blessings—literally. Count your abundance of real relationships, resources, talents, and treasures. Now find where you can do the most good and go do it. Even the smallest gestures can make a big difference.

Attitude #3: If You Want More, Give More

On the Leadership TV channel, there are a lot of winners and very few losers. Why? Leaders have a different attitude about a very fundamental aspect of life. Simply stated, leaders believe there is more than enough to go around, so they don't have to get ahead at someone else's expense. In their life's experiences, they have realized just how much the adage "It is better to give than receive" comes true, and they put it into practice. They have an attitude of abundance that allows them to win by giving, fostering others to do well, and sharing what they have.

At first, this may seem like a paradox, and it could even be challenging for some of us to embrace. After all, how can we end up having more if we are giving more away? Lee Brower, author of *The Brower Quadrant*, provides the answer: "It's enough to recognize that we live in an abundant world, and that when our hand is open to give, it's most open to receive."[3] Take a moment to contemplate that statement. When we open our hands, hearts, and even heads to give, we are allowing ourselves to receive the joy and satisfaction that comes from being a part of someone else's success. This isn't about just donating money to a charity; this is about sharing the various abundances in your life with others. This is the start of building and living a legacy.

Clearly, for many, this shift in focus from growing ourselves to growing others represents a significant change. How can this change be attempted, even embraced, especially in the competitive world we live in? There needs to be a sense of joy in watching others succeed rather than a sense of selfishness in trying to ensure you are the winner. It isn't a winner-take-all world, and we have to fight the temptation to make it that way. We don't obtain our dreams at the expense of others. There is no monopoly on ideal futures.

The rules in a leader's world are that everyone can win. The more we help others achieve what they want in life, the more likely we will achieve what *we* want in life. In other words, give more to get more. It is a winning formula. Imagine everyone adopting this attitude. What a great change! It is an attitude that you must adopt as a personal leader. It is a key attitude that will propel you in the direction of your ideal future.

Adopting the attitudes in this chapter will immediately decrease the amount of trauma and drama in your life. It's like switching off the television and discovering that an entirely different reality exists. In this reality, we can all win; we can all reach our ideal future. The reality of a leader's world is a choice. The path to personal leadership is there for the taking.

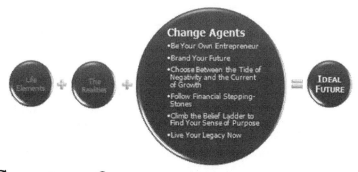

Section 3
CHANGE AGENTS

To follow the path to your ideal future, you must accept and act on a final set of factors in your equation: your change agents. This isn't a process that should be taken lightly. Change isn't easy. It takes effort, perseverance, and a level of willingness that will be tested. All in all, it is a process that is far easier said than done—yet to reach a high level of personal leadership, you must successfully manage it.

You have your foundation of life elements set. The realities are fully comprehended and brought into alignment with your expectations. To successfully reach your ideal future, you must now employ change agents that are designed to put your plans into action.

Fittingly, change starts with becoming your own entrepreneur. Thinking and acting like an entrepreneur will help you to create a vision of your ideal future as well as bring it to fruition. Along the way, you must accept that the brand you embrace will help you to accurately represent yourself to others. Progress will stall, however, until you turn the tide of negativity so it doesn't hold you back any longer. Using the knowledge you gained in your personal financial element, you have a financial plan in place to make your ideal future obtainable. Using your change agents, you will lift yourself to a higher level and finally leave a legacy that you have fully lived. Only when you accept responsibility for your own changes will you be empowered to reach your ideal future.

Authors' note: In order to really illustrate the power of change agents, at the end of every chapter in this section we have included our own personal stories. We hope you enjoy them and, even more importantly, are inspired by them. There is no reason for anyone to avoid change. We are living proof that it is truly possible.

CHAPTER 9

Be Your Own Entrepreneur

Who do you picture when someone mentions the word *entrepreneur*? Do you think about supersuccessful and highly visible businesspeople like Steve Jobs, Sir Richard Branson, Mark Zuckerberg, or anyone else who started with very little and built a vast empire? Maybe your mind recalls something about the teenage entrepreneur who became a millionaire from a problem he wanted to solve or small-business owners who have achieved local success. All of these represent facets of entrepreneurship and are valid references. Usually, these individuals have managed to make something out of seemingly nothing. Yet there is one more type of entrepreneur that hardly ever comes to mind: you! Have you ever considered that you, yourself, are the entrepreneur of your own life?

Entrepreneurs are people of great initiative. An incredible sense of purpose leads them to take on challenges and risks knowing that sometimes they will fail. Nothing can hold them back from what is needed to achieve their goals. Failures aren't viewed as setbacks; instead, they become learning foundations for the next attempts.

In tackling their initiatives, entrepreneurs will develop a vision, discover the gaps, creatively come up with solutions for ordinary problems, and rely more on action than words. They know who to turn to for help and usually don't let much stand in their way of success. Ultimately, there is an ability to judge the risks versus the rewards and a willingness to take necessary chances. Entrepreneurs' outcomes might not be completely as first planned, but ultimately they will be successful.

Now imagine your life if you were to tap into those same attributes. If you were to use just four steps—create a vision, discover the gaps, develop creative solutions, and act on the opportunities—you would be creating your own future road map. You would be taking the initiative and calculated risks you need to take to reach your ideal future.

Entrepreneurship is the first of the change agents because the characteristics of an entrepreneur are also at the heart of personal leadership. Once you capture them for yourself, you will capture the mind-set needed for the rest of the change agents.

> **Entrepreneurial Tip**
> Learn from the best! There are many articles and books written by entrepreneurs. Some have even taken to video blogging. Pick a few and research them. Find out how they have gotten so far in life and learn their secrets. The more you learn, the more you will understand how to apply their strategies to your own life.

Create a Vision

Entrepreneurs are often referred to as visionaries. Their point of view about the paths ahead are unique. They have the uncanny ability to see gems where others see ugly rocks. Some might even say everything they touch turns to gold. That is the wrong way to look at it. It makes it sound much easier than it really is.

The visionary talent that entrepreneurs possess is simply a matter of diligently searching through ugly rocks until they find the right perspective to make the gold appear. They actually become very fixated on their vision and the future it promises. This focus can be all-consuming and really frustrate those around them. It might even bring about harder times and more difficult choices. Yet entrepreneurs will not stop looking until they are successful. They persevere through the difficulties that have caused so many others to simply give up hope. Even after success comes, entrepreneurs will keep pushing new boundaries and developing more ideas.

It may be hard to imagine, yet this perseverance is a key characteristic of entrepreneurs. They're not about being satisfied with what has been accomplished; their focus remains on achieving the ideal. Now turn this approach back on yourself. How does this relate to personal leadership, your equation, and your ideal future? Do you have a clear vision of your ideal future? If not, what is stopping you from creating it?

At the end of this book's introduction, there was a Move into Action tool for envisioning your ideal future. Now is the time to really take it up a notch and begin to apply the entrepreneurial process to yourself. What are the items your ideal future holds? Did you dream big enough? Take another look at your vision for your ideal future. If you've previously created a bucket list, a leap list, or whatever you choose to call it, did those items make it into your ideal future? Consider the following as you take this step:

- What do you want for yourself, your family, your career, and your life? Visualize your hopes, goals, and dreams. Be creative, and be passionate—it is your life, after all. Include those who are most important to you in the process. In creating this initial vision, go straight for the gold. The time to search the ugly rocks will come later; for now, just focus on what the gold looks like.

- Get out of your comfort zone. If you have a partner, work with him or her to do the same. Be open and trusting. If you don't have a life partner, ask a trusted mentor to work with you. No one has to go it alone. Find someone to help. Just ask someone.

- Accept that you won't accomplish everything. That's okay—list it anyway. You are developing a vision and your ideal future is coming into focus.

Once your list is as complete as it's going to be—and it should never be totally complete—you will begin to move on to uncovering the gaps.

> *Do not be embarrassed by your failures,*
> *learn from them and start again.*
> *—Sir Richard Branson*

▨ Discover the Gaps

Entrepreneurs seem to have a magical way of seeing what is needed to fulfill the vision they have created. We know that life isn't magical or easy, though. Not everything is always 100 percent ready to go. Not everything lines up perfectly to execute the vision that has been created. Yet entrepreneurs are successful. Their vision works because they don't let the challenges in their vision scare them away. Entrepreneurs work hard to figure out how to take the challenges and turn them into opportunities. They discover the gaps. In creating your vision, you will need to do the same.

First, find your focus by filtering your ideal future list through the life factors and the realities. Determine what can and should be accomplished. Take the low-hanging-fruit approach and tackle some of the easier items first. It will help you gain confidence in your initiatives and increase your momentum.

Next, determine what calculated risks you can tolerate and take them. After your ideal future list has been prioritized, look at the top items and determine what is standing in the way of accomplishing them. These missing pieces are the gaps standing between your life today and your life in the ideal future. Think about what needs more development. What are the challenges associated with the gaps? This is the moment of courage. It takes courage to face the truth.

For example, let's look at a situation involving a life element. For years, you have been spinning your wheels at work. It seems that you're always passed over and others are going further faster. The vision is that you have decided it is your time. You are going to do what it takes to advance your career to the next level. Whether it is for the money, prestige, or just the need to advance yourself, you want that promotion.

Great! Now, the goal is to identify anything that is missing from your equation and address it. Why *hasn't* it been you? Let's assume further education is needed. The job promotion you would like requires an advanced college degree you do not have. This is the gap that stands between where you are today and your vision of achieving the promotion that will bring you another step closer to your ideal future.

College is expensive, and the cost might seem prohibitive. Life is already frantic enough, and you feel like you just don't have the time. A lack of time and the steep cost are components of this gap. For many, facing up to the gap is where the doubt comes in. Quickly concluding that the gap is too big to ever be closed gets you nowhere. This is where you really need that entrepreneurial spirit.

Do not fear gaps—embrace them. Understanding what gaps are made of is an important milestone. Whether you realize it or not, you have made a big step forward; you know what you want, and you understand what is missing. Now you're ready to find a way to fill those gaps.

▨ Develop Creative Solutions

The next step for entrepreneurs comes after they have identified the components of the gap. They have their vision, and they know what the gaps are. It is now time to figure out how to leap across those gaps. Entrepreneurs know there just has to be solution for a problem somehow, somewhere. Just as with creating the vision, when it comes to the creative solution, the entrepreneur is relentless in pursuit of the answer.

Here is the real secret: entrepreneurs may not have the creativity to come up with the solution by themselves, but they know who does. Their charm, enthusiasm, passion—whatever it is—draws the best of the best into their sphere, particularly those who can do something they can't. Entrepreneurs store this information and use it for the maximum benefit. When the time is right, they know who to ask for help.

Entrepreneurs have another secret that people might not immediately realize: they use the positives to push forward and the negatives to redirect. Nothing is taken as a personal affront when they listen to their true advisers. They know all advice is meant for the greater good. When you have that kind of honesty and acceptance, it actually frees you to be creative. There's a huge roadblock buster, and it's known as getting help.

Going back to our college dilemma, your vision is to achieve career advancement, and the gap is the need for an advanced college education. Finding the time and money to go back to college is the key to bridging this gap. This is a time for courage. This is a time to take risks. Accept that there are boundaries you will have to continually push. Don't worry about them, just dig in—and start with something simple.

Be creative in your solutions and look at every possible avenue. In our example, you might take an online course to test the waters to see if you can handle college work again and if you can fit it in your schedule. The best approach would be to take a required class that really interests you. Review your calendar to determine what activities could be dropped, at least while you're in school, to gain more time. They may not be easy decisions, and you might have to put things you really like aside. Remember that entrepreneurial spirit. You are filling the gaps.

Personally, at these moments, we like to remind ourselves that our sacrifices now are for the greater good later. Don't give up because you're worried, don't have time, or can't afford it. Try everything you can think of and reach out to everyone possible for help with your creative solutions.

How often do we hear or say, "I wish I could think of something like that" or "I am just not the creative type." These are such self-imposed roadblocks. While you might not have the answers needed to reach your vision, you can always ask someone you admire to talk a problem or issue through with you. Debate and discuss. Get multiple perspectives and absorb the ideas. Once you begin to feed off those who are truly trying to help you, you will take the next step in your personal leadership and become your own entrepreneur. You will find creative solutions to ordinary problems.

▇ Act on the Opportunities

You are now at the final phase. You built the vision, identified the gaps, and found solutions to the roadblocks that kept you from moving forward. What else is there? What are you waiting for? The answer should be, "Nothing." It's time for action. Put yourself into forward motion by setting your goals, listing your priorities, and making your action plans. If you need to, find someone who can mentor you and keep you moving forward.

Don't procrastinate, and don't talk about what you're going to do. Don't even think about how successful you will be someday. Take one step at a time and just get the job done. Entrepreneurs talk after the actions are completed, not before. Take their approach and work quietly on your life's innovations.

Until you put your words into action and experience successes and failures; until you do everything you can to nurture your ideas into fruition and still try more; and until you have been on a roller coaster and would do it all again, only then will you put your words into actions and embrace the entrepreneurial spirit needed to tear down roadblocks. Adopt the mind-set of embracing change. While it seems deceptively simple, accepting the challenge of change is the foundation of this factor of your equation. It is the lifeblood of an entrepreneur, and you need to tap into that spirit to face the upcoming change agents that will be so crucial in achieving your ideal future.

▰ Our Story: Dream Day

In this chapter, we discussed being your own entrepreneur, and it is a concept we have embraced throughout our entire relationship. Even in the earliest days of dating, we would make a list of all the activities we wanted to do in the short upstate New York summers. As we grew closer, the plans became bigger, and we always tried to set the vision of what our future life together would be like. Little did we know, this very approach would lead us to write this book! Here is a quick story of one of our dream days, and we hope it inspires you to plan one of your own.

For this dream day, we realized we needed to get out of our rut, so we took a long ride through the Adirondack Mountains. We were in the middle of some real challenges and knew we needed to clear our heads to be able to create new visions. Rather than jump right into it, after the first section of driving, we stopped at an inn we'd always wanted to go to for lunch. After the nice break, we continued a long and winding drive with breathtaking views. Talk about creating a vision! Finally, we reached a favorite small town with a lake that literally glittered like diamonds. It was beautiful, majestic, and awe-inspiring.

We sat on a dock and separately wrote our lists. As always, anything and everything we wanted could be listed, with no restrictions. This allowed us to be completely honest and open with each other. Once the lists were done, we shared them, discussed them, and merged them into a master list for our life. As our own entrepreneurs, we created an updated vision.

From there, it was almost easy to break the lists into one-year, two-year, longer-priority, and wish-list items. This is where we recognized gaps involving time and money. Things that could be accomplished easily were given priority. Items that required additional resources were slotted in when we thought we could realistically accomplish them. Within a very short time—an hour at most—we had our vision and some idea of the gaps.

When we returned home, as part of the process, we reviewed our lists with one of our mentors for her input. It was time for the creative solutions. She helped us find clarity on a few small items and courage for a few of the larger undertakings. Some of these conversations were not easy, but the trust and ultimate fulfillment that came from them can't be understated. We were so much further ahead in our efforts.

As for the action part, the one- and two-year goals have long since been completed. We are currently working on some of the longer priorities and have added more goals along the way. There are wish-list items we may never achieve, and that is okay. Those items are still listed, because while we know they may not be obtainable, we still have the ability to dream.

A final note: During this process, the care and concern we had for each other's needs was readily apparent, and there was no hint of selfishness. There was no need—we trusted each other with our own vulnerability and knew that trust was well placed. It was truly one of the best days of our married life. We dreamed it, and we are living proof of the results.

CHAPTER 10

Brand Your Future

When you're asked to think of a brand, do you think of Apple, Nike, Starbucks, or another of the millions of commercial brands in the world today? Whichever you just chose, chances are you are attracted to it because the company has spent countless hours and dollars developing and promoting a particular message. It has cultivated a certain appeal that is drawing you to name that particular brand.

Can you articulate your personal brand as well and as clearly as those commercial companies? How much time and effort have you spent cultivating it? Managing your personal brand is strikingly similar to managing a large commercial enterprise. In actively managing your personal brand, you are creating a magnetic force with positive and negative components. You must embrace the concept that a brand is a powerful change agent that will help you reach your ideal future.

There Is No Escaping It: You Have a Brand

Your brand is how everyone perceives you. It is uniquely yours, whether you want it or not. It is something you will never have full control over, because it comes down to how others receive and interpret your message. This is a very important point. Your brand is not what you say it is, it is what others see it as.

Understanding that what others think forms your personal brand is an important concept. We recall discussing personal brand with a college student who struggled with interpersonal relationships. When we mentioned personal brand to her, she strongly stated, "I don't care what anyone else thinks of me!" Larry G. Linne and Patrick Sitkins address this exact reaction in their brand management book *Brand Aid*. So many people have the attitude "If someone doesn't like me, that's his problem." Linne and Sitkins state that if you're looking for a job, working toward a promotion, or trying to achieve any other goal in your life, the problem other people have with you is going to be yours, not theirs.[4]

Clearly, the student we spoke to didn't get that message. When she said she didn't care, she was actually putting up a wall between her and anyone who ever might want to help her. Maybe, someday, she will figure out that this mind-set is to her great detriment. More than likely, she will wallow in her life wondering why it's so hard to achieve her goals. Yes, it matters a great deal what others think of you—and how much effort you make to engage them in your brand.

A lot of different people receive your brand message, including your family, friends, coworkers, and everyone who comes in contact with you through social media. You might not fully know what others genuinely think of you. Rarely do they just walk up and give it to you straight.

A good first step to developing the self-awareness that is crucial to your brand is a survey. Businesses conduct surveys on a continual basis and in a variety of ways. Why do they spend so much time and resources on surveys? They do it to gather feedback they otherwise would never receive. Oftentimes, they are collecting information about consumer perceptions and experiences, which are the crucial elements that constitute "brand." These companies are quick to take action and adjust their messaging as needed.

Taking a cue from commercial brands, list at least three words that best describe your personal view of yourself. These are part of your desired brand definition. Next, ask others what they genuinely think of you. As we have noted several times already in this book, others know more about you than you realize. It might even be interesting to learn what they see in your future. You can ask those around you—perhaps your manager, coworkers, peers, friends, and family members. As with any survey, make sure you have a wide cross section of people. Include anyone who you trust to be completely candid in this process. Challenge them to use three words to describe you. These few words will help you to understand your current brand and how it aligns with your perceptions.

While the next section discusses the elements of a brand, you may want to ask people what their first impressions are or what they think of how you dress and communicate. Once you start comparing these responses to each other and then back to your own words, any differences should become readily apparent. While these are just opinions, the more you ask, the more you will see patterns emerge. Such patterns, good or bad, will give you the insight you need to further hone your personal brand.

Personal brand is a change agent that is often ignored, underutilized, or completely misunderstood. Realizing what people think so you can articulate your brand is the first step to leveraging its power. With this newfound brand awareness, you too can reap all that a personal brand has to offer, including its power to propel you toward your ideal future.

◼ Your Visible Brand Elements

Knowing the elements that constitute your brand gives you a place to start when you want to change directions. What are the elements of a great personal brand—clothing, voice, vocabulary, body language, sensitivity to others? Yes to all of these—plus so much more, including the element of understanding and adapting to the audience. Brand is a package of communication skills, including physical, emotional, and social aspects. Your brand has to have a cohesive communication package.

If you've done the survey in the first section, look at the first impression others have of you. These insights might include what people think about how you dress, the words you use, how you communicate, and so on. This first impression is either going to foster your efforts or thwart them. What do people currently see? Does this match the brand you want for yourself?

Next, search for yourself on the Internet. Are your social media profiles consistent with the words you identified as your brand? You may focus LinkedIn on your professional brand, yet if you post damaging items on Facebook, the overall brand-communication package fails. It is far too easy to cross-reference between social media sites. Profile pictures, viewpoints, and other posts should be shared judiciously. Make sure your message is consistent across all channels, as well as in line with what you truly intend to portray. Social media, online content, and initial impressions are among the first visible elements of your brand.

Finally, consider how you interact. That is another element of a brand. You have more communication options than ever, including e-mail, phone, videoconferencing, and face-to-face meetings. Regardless of whether they searched you out on the Internet or not, the first time people communicate directly with you is a momentous occasion. It is an event that makes a powerful and lasting impression. Because there are so many aspects to consider, we have condensed those that are most important into a reference chart of your brand communication package:

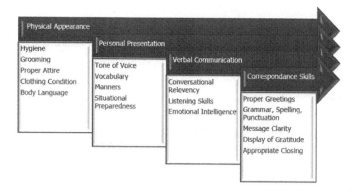

Each situation you encounter will be as unique as the people who are receiving the message. The interaction element of your personal brand communication package will need to be adapted and modified for the situation at hand.

There is one very important common element to all your interactions: how you make the other person feel. Over time, the actual words communicated in any situation will fade away, but the feeling will remain. Brand is much more emotional than intellectual, and you need to ensure that your interactions have some level of emotional connection. What will people remember from your interaction, and more importantly, what words would they use to describe you? The goal is to have those words correspond to the brand you're trying to portray—the words you wrote down for yourself. If you can successfully accomplish this, the complete connection has been made, and you have taken a giant leap toward developing your brand.

■ Brand Upkeep

As you change and your life moves forward with new experiences and goals, you'll want your brand to change along with it. It is inevitable that you will grow. Your brand as a twentysomething should be different from what it will likely be when you are a thirtysomething, fortysomething, and beyond. As you move through different stages of life, you will need to refine and update your brand on a regular basis. To do so, you should revisit your brand definition annually. Update the key words that define your desired brand. Consider whether your audience has changed. If it has, identify each new audience and the best methods of communication for reaching them. Keeping your desired brand definition up to date is a key element in proactively managing your brand communication package.

You'll need to monitor your brand continually. Seek feedback. Opportunities will present themselves to tap into understanding how others perceive you. Make the most of these opportunities. You may need to occasionally get this feedback by asking for it outright, whether via conversation or survey. Don't make the mistake of just assuming that once you have defined your desired brand, everyone is getting the message. Check on the effectiveness of your communication efforts often. Adjust those efforts as necessary based upon feedback received.

Finally, consider utilizing new methods to communicate your brand as they become available. Two hundred years ago, people communicated via verbal conversation or written letters. There weren't many options beyond that. Technology has radically changed how we communicate. Of course, you need to be savvy in your utilization of many different methods of communication, and overreliance on any one method may be detrimental. Be mindful of how the other person wants to be communicated to. Consider your options and keep the receiver in mind.

> **Brand Building Tip**
> What's old is new again. One of our favorite pieces of advice is to never underestimate the power of letter-writing. In a world that is drowning in e-mail, posts, and tweets, it is refreshing to receive a good old-fashioned handwritten card delivered by postage-bearing mail. It is one of our favorite ways to make an impression. The handwritten note is becoming ever more rare and valuable. Make it a treasured part of your brand.

It can take a long time to build your desired brand, yet that brand can be destroyed in a mere moment. We cannot emphasize strongly enough how fragile brands can be. Never let your guard down. One bad interaction can cascade and destroy years of brand-building efforts. Make your personal brand one of your greatest enablers in changing your equation. Be clear on what you want your brand to be and manage, manage, manage it some more. Take every opportunity to get a reading on how others perceive you. To reach your ideal future, you must be self-aware and make your brand an equation changer.

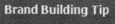 Don's Story: From Farm Boy to Executive

Let's start back where it all began: on the family farm in rural central New York state. There is a certain independence common among farmers. Growing up, I was never overly concerned about the way I was perceived. There was no great desire to be just like the coolest, most popular kids in school. Wearing exactly what they wore or doing everything they did just didn't seem all that important. Certainly I did not subscribe to the idea that image was everything.

My transition into the professional world didn't change my thinking much. There is a saying: "You can take the boy from the farm but not the farm from the boy." The saying really did apply to me. I remember I was in my second serious career, an IT professional, and my uniform of choice consisted of a white dress shirt, dark dress pants, and a conservative necktie. I'm sure that was what I was wearing when Roe joined the same company and met me. In fact, that was just about the only way she ever saw me—always in that white shirt and tie.

I was a little surprised as I got to know Roe and understand her perception of me. She would say, "Farm boy? What farm boy?" I actually think she doubted I owned any T-shirts or jeans. The point here is that people really see us as we present ourselves today, not as we may think of ourselves. I was still in the habit of thinking of myself as the farm kid in the white T-shirt and jeans, but times had changed.

Soon after moving to my next job and making somewhat of a career change—back to more finance and less IT—I connected with some career coaches. Brand awareness became a reality for me. For the first time, I started to discover how others really perceived me. This included the perceptions of a coach, Larry Linne, who I wasn't quite sure what to make of.

In one of our early coaching sessions, after hearing his perception of me, I set out to tell him he was wrong.

Larry's reply to me was, "You're defensive."

I replied, "Defensive, me? Who are you calling defensive?"

Okay, he was right. I suppose it was both obvious and ironic; I was being defensive about being called defensive. His statement was eye-opening and ultimately a turning point in my career and life. The realities started to set in. First, I had a brand with some people that wasn't very positive, which was a difficult conclusion to accept. My mind was closed in some areas, and it clearly showed. Second, unless I addressed it, this would have negative implications for my career and life. After all, I wasn't asking or accepting anybody's help because I was convinced I already knew all the answers. Lastly, defensive people aren't very coachable. If you aren't open to coaching, you aren't open to change. Clearly my mind-set about brand had to shift before I could get the insights needed to reach my own ideal future.

Upon additional reflection, acceptance started to take hold. I concluded that there was nothing to be defensive about. Everyone was entitled to his own perception. If I didn't like what others saw and experienced in their interactions with me, it was my fault, not theirs. My coach's comments weren't meant to tear me down; I was the one who was doing that by taking them in such a way. His candor was meant to be a learning tool for me to use to grow my brand. It was entirely up to me to put that tool to good use.

That conversation with Larry was many years ago now, yet I consider it to have been one of the most important. It was a pivotal time for me in taking ownership of my brand. As I grew more and more in awareness of my brand, our relationship grew. My openness to his expertise propelled me further than I ever anticipated. Along the way, Larry even conducted a personal survey on my behalf so people I worked with could feel completely secure in telling their true perceptions of me and my work. The results were reflective of my positivity and professionalism. What I really learned from the survey exercise was that the things I was trying to emphasize really came through in their perceptions.

Overall, my brand management has paid off and continues to do so. The farm boy of old is the successful executive of today. I put a lot of consideration into what I wear, what I say, who I associate with, and how I make others feel. Long gone are the thoughts of T-shirts and jeans. While I'm very proud to have the farm boy mentality within me, it certainly doesn't make up much of my brand. Now it's about others thinking, "Yeah, I see an incredible leader." I'm confident I can achieve whatever career goals I set for myself as my brand management propels me to my ideal future.

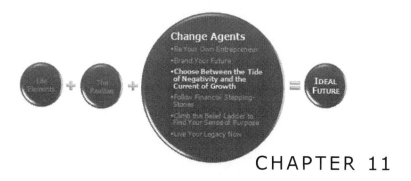

Choose between the Tide of Negativity and the Current of Growth

How often do we see children who have experienced pain become terrified of the source afterward? It may be something as simple as soap in their eyes from a bath, a bee sting, or a shot at the doctor's office. Anything that causes injury, no matter how big or small, becomes a source of anxiety and stress. Because of the fear that has built up, the smallest pinprick becomes inflated to the point of absolute hysterics. After much cajoling, many bribes, and even a few threats, the injury is over—usually with the parent saying; "See, that wasn't so bad!" The child shuffles away, usually sniffling, refusing to acknowledge that it was anything but complete torture.

As we grow into adulthood, while the lingering memory may remain, we have learned that pain is fleeting because we understand the cause. As we matured, so did our understanding that a little pain from a shot prevented us from a much more serious illness. Even more ironic, as grown-ups we become the ones who end up saying, "See, that wasn't so bad." Unfortunately, the same may not be said about the more complex situations we face as adults.

The more we experience in life, the more it impacts our perspective. It is very natural for us to take something bad that may have happened once and project it forward to something that will always occur. It becomes a trap from which we cannot escape. Even more alarming is that we allow this negative energy to get more and more swept up in the issues of those around us. As we complain and gripe, they feel open to do the same. Their wars become our battles and vice versa. The more we allow ourselves to be caught up in the tide of negativity, the more it takes our focus away from our ideal future.

It is easy to forget that the tide holds the current of growth. In the book *The Secret* by Rhonda Byrne, the "law of attraction" is explored. This concept illustrates how much better off people can be when they project positivity, for that is what they will receive back. Byrne writes, "What you are thinking now is creating your future life. You create your life with your thoughts. Because you are always thinking, you are always creating. What you think about the most or focus on the most, is what will appear as your life."[5]

Oftentimes it is the uncomfortable or painful situations that bring the most growth and provide us with new strengths. A life in which the goal is to minimize pain and discomfort becomes a life of stagnation, a life without growth. No wonder there is so much frustration when people talk about not bothering with hopes and dreams. In their world, the ideal future seems unattainable. It isn't, though, especially if we look to the positives in our lives. It is time to put the trap of past negatives behind us and avoid the tide of negativity that surrounds us. We need to instead enjoy the water and unburden ourselves of the anchors that are holding us down. By doing so, we will actively choose the current of growth.

▰ Break Free from the Trap of Past Negatives

In our adult relationships and encounters, when we experience something negative, the pain is generally deeper and much longer lasting. We can be caught in a trap of negativity, and it can plague us for years. In reflecting on this, we can honestly say that the old adage of "once bitten, twice shy" might well be "once bitten, forever shy, fearful, angry, betrayed, and hurt."

As the situation swirls in our thoughts, a small infraction can become an all-out war. We develop full conversations around what we will say next time, without any resolution with the offending party in the here and now. The trap of negativity is set.

When we are caught in the trap, the mind-set is clear to us, and we vow we will never do that again. We convince ourselves that trying will only bring about more struggle, more strife, and ultimately more failure. This is clearly evident when you hear someone say, "Why should I bother?" or "I give up, it never goes right for me anyways." Instead of being open to possibilities, we immediately shut down any hope for a good outcome. At that moment, there is no one who has it worse than us. The roadblock is up, and it is completely impenetrable. We're trapped in negativity, yet it is our own doing.

There is only one way out, and we are the only ones who can truly free ourselves. First and foremost, we have to change our internal conversation and begin to focus more on what we want to attract to ourselves. By doing so, we will begin to repel all those negative thoughts that have trapped us in the past. We must take every negative thought we have and turn it around to a positive perspective. This isn't easy, and it does take practice. The graphic below will help you get started.

> *Breaking free from the trap means you are taking your negative situations and turning them into positive outcomes to attract your ideal future.*

NEGATIVE SITUATIONS

- After having a bad meal at a favorite restaurant, you swear you will never go back.
- Someone snaps at you, and you immediately become angry with that person.
- After a tough breakup, you declare that you will never date again.
- Losing your job makes you think you will never find another job.
- You second-guess your past decisions and blame yourself for the choices you shoulda, woulda, coulda made.
- Betrayed by someone, or many people, you absolutely refuse to trust anyone again.

POSITIVE OUTCOMES

- Try the restaurant again and look for a pattern before you automatically assume the worst.
- Stop and ask the person who snapped at you what is going on, if it is about you, address it immediately; if it isn't, empathize with them to build a stronger connection.
- Think about the qualities you liked best from the time with your ex and use them as a foundation for your next, and perhaps even better, relationship.
- Instead of focusing on the job loss, view it as an opportunity to try new career paths.
- Take those situations and look at just how much you have grown since then. Give yourself credit for the positive learning you have accomplished.
- Forgive the betrayer and move on. Don't let them ruin the greatness that comes from being able to trust. The roadblock is solely your creation. Take it down.

When we choose to implement a positive perspective, we are growing from the negative scenarios life is bound to throw at us. When we choose to look at the positive outcomes and recognize the abundance around us, we are allowing ourselves to attract what we want for our ideal future.

Positivity Tip

It is impossible to be negative and positive at the same time. When you are in a negative mind-set, change your internal conversation. Counter a negative thought with the positive aspect. The more you change the perspective internally, the more you will change your external view.

◼ Don't Get Swept into the Tide of Negativity

It might be tempting to think that we're immune from the mood of the people around us, but the fact is that groups can influence how we feel and what we do. We're absorbing all sorts of emotions from other people because we all have some level of empathy. If another person is exhibiting joy, we feel more joyous. If we are around someone who is very stressed for any length of time, we likely will feel more stressed at the end of the encounter. The more highly empathetic you are, the higher the rate of absorption.

Through this process of emotional absorption, we take ownership of other people's issues. Often as someone else struggles with something, we step in and internalize it as our own. It may not be anything we will ever have to face, but that doesn't matter. Other people's issues becomes a real factor in our lives. In all actuality, their weaknesses become our own. This negative stance doesn't allow us to realize the strengths that exist in our own personal experiences, talents, and even self-confidence. Instead, we have elevated their adverse experiences above our own positive abilities. The consequence of these negative emotions is that they become a roadblock to our willingness to change.

The people around us affect what we are willing to do too, because it seems too hard to move away from the crowd. Our individual apprehensions and fears multiply very quickly when we are with others. In most cases, people find strength in numbers and don't want to be caught out alone. While a few brave souls may be willing to dive into the challenge, the natural tendency is to stay within the safety of the group.

The mind-set behind this inaction is fairly transparent. If we put ourselves out there, we may fail in front of the group. We become certain that we will look weak and risk ridicule. No, no, no ... we refuse to be so vulnerable. It is far better to move with the group even if it means staying with the negative tide. It is best not to even attempt the challenge. No good could come from diving headfirst into the unknown.

As the brave ones, the leaders, go off to face the challenge, those who are left behind start rationalizing. Statements like "He's crazy" or "It is easy for her because ..." grow louder and louder. This is when the negativity really starts to gain momentum. More and more voices chime in, and the statements become even harsher. Rather than praising those who dared to try, the group transforms it back as foolish insanity by the leaders. The tide of negativity has churned into a full-blown rip current. The longer this continues, the harder it is to pull away. People so caught up in the riptide get swept out to the ocean of nothingness and drown in negativity.

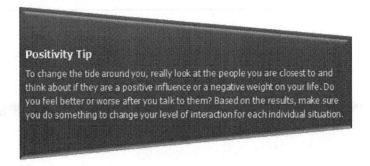

Positivity Tip

To change the tide around you, really look at the people you are closest to and think about if they are a positive influence or a negative weight on your life. Do you feel better or worse after you talk to them? Based on the results, make sure you do something to change your level of interaction for each individual situation.

In striving for your ideal future, you must become one of the brave leaders who goes off to face the challenges and break the tide.

In doing so, you can and should protect yourself from absorbing others' negative energy. To accomplish this, you must first become aware of how and when this influence is happening. Pay attention to those who seem to be bringing you down the most. Once you have that awareness, you can employ a number of techniques to prevent or minimize the absorption of negative energy.

Dr. Judith Orloff is a best-selling author who has many insights into the topics of stress and negativity. On her website, www.drjudithorloff.com, she has many resources available. Her techniques include the following:

1. Walk away. Creating a physical distance of at least twenty feet will prevent you from absorbing other people's negativity.
2. Meditate. Daily meditation will help you refocus and maintain your desired attitude, minimizing the harmful effects of negative absorption.[6]

Developing awareness of the negative energy around you and protecting yourself from it will assist you in maintaining positivity and all its benefits.

Dr. Orloff's techniques are a great starting point for the change you need to tear down this roadblock. With it gone, you will begin to recognize that approaching new, even uncertain experiences with positivity allows you to increase your personal strength. The added benefit of this process is that positive people attract other positive people. Great leaders break away from the tide of negativity and bravely venture into the unknown. They choose a different ocean to swim in and will turn away from those whose sole purpose is to bring others down. These personal leaders build on their own strengths by being with others who will enhance their lives, not those who would tear them down. By developing our personal leadership and being brave, we attract positives. We join others who might help us on our journey, and in return, we get to help them. Together, we will create a tide pool of change.

It's better to hang out with people better than you. Pick out associates whose behavior is better than yours and you'll drift in that direction.
—*Warren Buffet*

▨ Enjoy the Water

Successful leaders have a way of taking the negatives and turning them into positive growth experiences. They don't fear the water, the potential rip currents, and the fact that drowning is only one of many dangers of swimming in the ocean, because they know that inaction is far, far worse than the negative consequences they might encounter by taking action. All too often, fear of potential negative consequences can put you in safe mode. This is a mindset of minimizing risk. It is choosing to stay in your comfort zone where you feel the safest so you avoid negative consequences by not getting involved. However, there is no forward progress and little growth. It is a false sense of safety.

Leaders continually choose to live differently from others because they actually embrace being uncomfortable. Why should we follow them and push ourselves too? Simply because that is when and where personal growth happens. Discomfort and, yes, even facing some negativity in our lives means we can grow to our goals.

When you experience something negative, whether from your own fault or someone else's, step back and do a little analysis. Think about what you learned from the experience and how you can apply this newfound knowledge to future situations. Give yourself permission to move on and realize how much this perceived failure has actually made you smarter and stronger. You are now better prepared to face similar situations in the future. When you do so, you are raising your level of personal leadership. Use negative outcomes to empower you as someone who is stronger for their journey to the ideal future.

▧ Relieve Yourself of the Anchors: Forgive

Negative experiences are anchors that deplete our energy and distract our focus away from the future. This weight is usually invisible, and those who carry it are often totally unaware of it. A scale reveals our weight, our body mass. Unfortunately, there is no scale anyone can simply step on to get a reading of the heavy, negative anchors they are continually lugging. If such a scale existed, more would take action against this terrible affliction.

Too many people believe that they should not give forgiveness, as the offending party is deemed unworthy of it. Surprisingly, forgiveness has nothing to do with anyone being worthy. Let's understand who truly benefits from giving forgiveness. Well, both the giver and receiver of it benefit. Who benefits first? Who benefits most? It is the giver! Forgiveness is the gift we give ourselves first.

Consider what happens when we forgive someone. All that negativity and the heavy anchor we were carrying are removed from our lives. Immediately, we have more energy, and our focus shifts toward the future. This happens regardless of whether the forgiveness is accepted by the offending party. In fact, it doesn't even have to be communicated. The benefits of forgiveness can be fully realized as long as you forgive with your heart.

Do not confuse forgiveness with forgetting what happened in the first place. Forgiveness is a conscious decision to let go and doesn't imply that the situation should be completely forgotten. It is important to learn from the events of the past so as to not repeat them. Forgetting would lead to us to be vulnerable to similar situations that would hurt us in the future. Forgiveness does not allow us to forget what has happened; it allows us to simply let go of all the negativity and associated weight.

If forgiveness is a gift we give ourselves first, what is preventing you from giving it freely? The answer should be "nothing." Go ahead and forgive someone who you feel has wronged you in the past. Afterward, concentrate on how much better you feel. Do you want more of this same great feeling? All you have to do to get more is forgive more. It really is that simple and powerful. You'll experience so much more positivity and joy in your life the more you give yourself the gift of forgiveness.

Roe's Experience with the Tides of Negativity

The concepts of this chapter can be illustrated by a public speaking exercise from my time as an adjunct instructor at a local community college. The assignment was for students to present an elevator pitch about themselves. For the assignment, all the students had to do was pretend to be on an elevator with a businessperson they admired and ask for an appointment to discuss possible internship opportunities. There were really only four brief statements the student needed to make. These statements were:

1. "Please allow me to introduce myself ..."
2. "Currently, I am studying ..."
3. "I admire you because ..."
4. "Would you meet with me to discuss ..."

The students were given a week to practice and prepare. It was a simple exercise in front of their peers. This was not a high-stakes situation. The risk of failure was low. The importance of the assignment was to prepare for public speaking, something all of us need to be able to do in real life. Putting ourselves out there by taking a chance at something is how we get closer to our ideal future. We cannot have roadblocks up and engage others at the same time. It just doesn't work. Engagement requires us to be open, even vulnerable, so others see the true person and demonstrate courage in the face of the unknown.

After the assignment was announced, almost immediately the groans, whispers, and uncomfortable shuffling began. Some students even loudly announced that there was no way they would stand in front of the class. The negative tide was in full force as more and more joined in. It became a frenzy of "No" or "I can't speak in front of people"—even though they were more than happy to be vocal when in their seats. They were sure they would fail, and the irony was that the only real way to fail would be to not attempt the assignment.

Many students stayed after class to plead their case. The excuses were always the same: "I am too shy" or "I am too nervous" or "I hate speaking in front of people." The begging and pleading were to no avail, of course. If they had only put that energy into the assignment, they would have been so much better off.

The presentation day arrived, and some students did indeed take a zero for the assignment by not even coming to class. Most shuffled in as if they were on death row. There were even tearful pleas and panic attacks. Most of the students worked themselves into a frenzy of negativity. Now remember—these are college students! Just how many horrible, terrifying public-speaking experiences had they really had? Probably very few, if any; yet the roadblocks were up. There was no reason for it, but most of the students were absolutely convinced that it was just going to be the worst class ever.

As the first brave student took the stage—or in this case, just walked to the front of the classroom—the nervous energy was everywhere. The student rushed through his pitch; he was just trying to make the time fly, the whole thirty seconds of it. Then there was silence. The class looked around ... no one had died yet. There might have been one or two hints or notes for improvement, but no negative repercussions. It was not as bad as everyone made it out to be.

This scenario played out for almost every student. Some were braver than others and were happy to go next. Others waited in anxious dread. There were still students who complained and tried to refuse because they imagined their fellow students would laugh and mock them. Once their turn was over, however, they realized that the other students were encouraging and offered praise. The whole point of the exercise was just to open a door for them. It showed them the roadblock was not real.

In the end, everyone who attempted it survived the assignment, some better than others. Instead of dreading or fearing it, the class should have embraced the opportunity to practice for the future. Those students who were not brave enough to try the assignment missed a valuable opportunity to develop themselves. Those students who completed the assignment, the ones who were brave enough to at least make the attempt, were given a reward for their efforts. Everyone who participated received a full 100 percent on the assignment because it was never about their abilities; it was always about rewarding their courage.

CHAPTER 12

Follow Financial Stepping-Stones

In chapter 4, you began the process of taking a reading of your financial life element. Now, as promised, it is time to put it to use and develop stepping-stones as a financial change agent. Your financial health has major implications for your ability to reach your ideal future. This aspect of personal leadership is a powerful change agent you must employ to reach your fullest potential.

Let's make an important distinction about the journey. The goal is not to become rich. The end result is about becoming financially well. Get used to hearing the term "financial wellness." Based on the number of apps, devices, and health food stores popping up everywhere, our society has become far more focused on the importance of physical wellness. Now the time has come for us to reach the same level of engagement with our financial wellness.

Far too many authors suggest that the solution to financial stress is to just make more money. As we noted in chapter 4, the likelihood is that there is just so much money you can make, and their message misses the mark. Our approach is to fully empower you to implement changes to your financial mind-set. When you do so, you will attain a higher level of financial wellness, which will bring you closer to reaching your ideal future.

To help you start on a better financial path, one that tackles these issues head on, we have developed key actions you can take. We'll start by doing a short checkup, and then we'll address the stepping-stones that break financial management into manageable tasks to help you reach your ideal future. Remember it is likely that your financial situation isn't unique. These are common stressors in people's lives, and they can be overcome. In fact, these eight stepping-stones apply universally, regardless of your current situation—your age, your amount of savings or debt, or much of anything else.

■ Eight Questions for Financial Health Awareness

Answer yes or no for each of the eight wellness questions below. Answer yes only if you have the item in place and have reviewed it within the past twelve months to assure it is up to date.

1. Do you have a monthly and annual budget that includes the amounts you need to pay down debt as well as save the desired amount for retirement? (You should have one from the chapter 4 exercise.)
2. Have you created a personal balance sheet that lists all your assets and their associated values as well as your liabilities, including all outstanding loans and credit card balances? (Again, you should have completed this at the end of chapter 4.)
3. Are you confident in your education and skill level so as to be able to make your own financial decisions?
4. Do you have an emergency fund in place that will cover you in the event of a job loss or large unexpected expense?

5. Do you know how much money you will need in order to retire at a specific age with your desired lifestyle? What is your plan to reach that amount?

6. What is your credit score, and are you actively managing it?

7. When was the last time you reviewed your insurance coverage, and is it enough to ensure appropriate coverage for all your assets?

8. Do you have an estate plan that includes a will, health care proxy, power of attorney, and life, disability, and long-term care insurance analysis?

Now tally up how many yes answers you have.

- *If you have eight yes answers*, you seem to be financially well. As you read through the rest of the chapter, consider how you intend to stay in that healthy state.

- *If you have six or seven yes answers*, you are passing but there is room for improvement. Focus on those "no" stepping-stones while still paying attention to those areas that are doing well.

- *If you have fewer than six yes answers*, you have more financial stress than you should. Don't despair, though; the stepping-stones are designed to be a prescription for your ailments. It will take awareness, accountability, and action to improve, but you can do it. There is no reason you can't tear down this roadblock and achieve your ideal future.

■ The Eight Stepping-Stones

Stone #1: Budget

If you didn't have a budget previously, we hope you built one after reading chapter 4. You cannot go further without knowing where your money goes. The budget helps you to allocate based on needs and will show you where modifications can be made.

Perhaps there is a wedding you are going to be in, and the cost is high. Instead of just piling on the credit card debt, use the budget as a decision-making tool. Looking at your overall picture might show that by cutting down on your entertainment expenses for a while, you can save the money needed. It may also help you determine that you have to turn down the opportunity or get a part-time job to defray the costs. Whatever the case may be, you are using solid, concrete facts and figures to make the decisions in your financial life. It is a proactive approach that sets the mortar for the rest of the stepping-stones.

Stone #2: Personal Balance Sheet

As we discussed in chapter 4, a balance sheet is a tool that helps you to know your total net worth. It is the next step after your budget because it shows the big picture of the amount of balance you have in your financial life. It is simply a financial inventory of everything you owe to others versus everything you own.

Are you leaning heavily on the debt side or more positively on the savings side? Knowing and tracking your financial net worth is another important step to reducing financial stress. In looking at it, you may realize that you aren't as prepared to purchase a house as you thought. While you may have enough for the down payment, combined with your budget picture, the information shows you are not ready to meet the larger monthly expenses associated with home ownership. Having the knowledge ahead of time allows you to make decisions that will reduce your financial stress instead of increasing it. In the end, you are empowering yourself to create an action plan for obtaining items that are a part of your ideal future.

Stone #3: Financial Education

Obtaining basic personal financial-management education is an absolute necessity. After all, we make financial decisions on a daily basis, so it is essential that you have a solid understanding of the basic principles of personal finance. Every time we reach into our wallets and pull out some cash, a debit card, or a credit card, we're making a financial transaction. The same is true each time we save money and deposit it into a savings account or perhaps invest it in a 401K or mutual fund. You can't stop and ask someone for financial advice before making each and every transaction; you have to take responsibility for making sound decisions most often on your own. There is just no substitute for being able to make your own knowledgeable financial decisions.

Unfortunately, it is very easy to get through high school and college without ever acquiring this most essential knowledge. If you're uncomfortable with such topics as budgeting, investing, and compound interest, or you have difficulty explaining how stocks and bonds are different, the best investment you can make is in your own personal financial education.

There is a plethora of sources of financial information, so it is important to find what works best for you. The following are some good ways to start to increasing your knowledge of personal finance:

- Pick up a couple of good personal finance books. We recommend:
  - *The Automatic Millionaire* by David Bach,[7] a great book to help you put your financial future on autopilot.

- o *I Will Teach You to Be Rich* by Ramit Sethi.[8] The book combines financial advice with real-world situations especially relevant to the millennial generation.
- o *The Investment Answer* by Daniel C. Goldie, CFA, CFP, and Gordon S. Murray.[9] Short and to the point, it offers a wealth of information about building an investment philosophy for the long term.
- Look into personal financial courses offered in your local area by community colleges and financial institutions.
- Online courses are readily available, many at no cost. Try visiting the Udemy website (www.udemy.com) and searching "personal finance."
- Talk to local financial advisers in your community. Explain your financial situation. If they can't help you, they'll likely be able to direct you to someone who can.

Knowledge of basic financial principles will serve as the foundation for your financial future. It will absolutely be one of the best investments you will ever make in yourself.

Financial Tip

"Pay yourself first." The money you pay others pays *their* future. The money you pay yourself pays the way to *your* ideal future. An easy way to stop this neglect is to get into a new habit—a habit of saving. Even if it is ten dollars a week to start, begin to build your emergency fund, your retirement savings, and eventually your special project money. Stop wondering where your paycheck goes and start building your resources.

Stone #4: Emergency Fund

By actively addressing the need to plan for potential emergencies, you're taking away some of the financial risks life will present. An emergency fund is just that: money set aside in case of an emergency. Although seemingly a simple concept, it's one that many people are not prepared to handle. According to a recent survey conducted by the Associated Press–NORC Centre for Public Research, two thirds of Americans would struggle to cover an unexpected $1,000 bill.[10] Sure, you might be able to borrow the money in a pinch, but you'll be at the mercy of the lender who is charging an interest rate of 10 percent, 20 percent, or more. Those payments can easily escalate, and as they do, so does your stress level. An emergency fund is essential to maintaining your financial health and keeping you in control of your finances rather than your creditors controlling you.

A good rule of thumb is to have an emergency fund equal to six months of your basic expenses. For example, if you spend $50,000 a year on living expenses and debt payments, an emergency fund of $25,000 would cover you in the event you had no income for six months. You want this $25,000 emergency fund to be readily available in cash savings or investments. It is your safe money that you can easily tap into without wrecking your retirement savings plan. Start saving toward that number now. This will give you peace of mind that you will be able to cope with unexpected events in life.

Building an emergency fund to cover six months of expenses may sound daunting, especially if you have little or no savings and not much extra income to build on. Don't be disheartened. Having a one-month emergency fund is better than none, and a two-month fund is better than one. To keep you motivated to save, track the growth of your emergency fund monthly. As it grows, think of the financial freedom you'll enjoy and the amount of stress that you won't have to endure. Your financial freedom and resulting peace of mind are priceless.

> *A big part of financial freedom is having your heart*
> *and mind free from worry about the what-ifs of life.*
> —*Suze Orman*

Stone #5: Retirement Plan

It may be ten years away, fifty years away, or anywhere in between, but someday, you probably hope to retire. The next step on the path to financial wellness is your retirement plan. Mostly gone are the days when people worked thirty years and left with a guaranteed monthly pension. Now it is up to you to plan and save for those so-called golden years. Unfortunately for far too many, they will be tarnished years with few resources and much stress. To avoid this pitfall, work on your retirement savings plan. As cliché as it may seem, you're never too young or too old.

In general, your retirement plan should indicate how much savings you will need to live your desired retirement. That picture will depend on the age you plan on stepping out of the work world and what you hope to accomplish in life after that point. How quickly you get there is also up to you. It can be a complex set of circumstances, yet there is help. Don't just contribute to a 401k or something similar and expect everything to work out fine. Increase your awareness by learning more or working with a professional. Hold yourself accountable to pay yourself first, save that retirement money, and create an action plan to reach your desired end result. Whether you realize it or not, your retirement is a part of your ideal future. Make sure you have created the ability to choose your own path.

Stone #6: Credit Score

A credit score is a number that indicates how easily you could repay a loan. Lenders use it to determine whether they will loan you money for an important purchase, and others can use it to determine the interest rate or even insurance rate you will receive. Your credit information is compiled by at least three organizations—Experian, Equifax, and Transunion—and the score is calculated from what is on that report. You can easily get your credit score from these company websites and even apps like Credit Karma. When you apply for a credit card, take out a car loan, or seek approval for a mortgage, the creditor will likely pull your credit report and credit score from at least one of the above three credit-reporting bureaus.

The credit report is a detailed history of all important credit transactions, including all of your current lines of credit available, how timely you are with payments, and how much you currently owe on them. Each credit bureau takes your credit information and summarizes it with a numerical score, generally a number between 300 and 850. The higher your credit score, the better. Good credit is generally considered a score of 700 or higher.

Managing your credit and ultimately your credit score is fairly straightforward. Here are some basic techniques that will keep your credit score moving higher:

- Pay your bills on time, every time. This includes credit card bills and all loan payments.
- Don't use all your available credit. Try to keep your actual credit used to 30 percent of all available credit. For example, if your credit card limits total $10,000, you should keep your utilization to approximately $3,000 or less.
- Credit scores improve with the amount of credit history available. The more experience you have making your

payments on time, generally the better your credit score will be.

- Don't apply for credit that you don't need. Keeping credit cards that you don't need or rarely use can be a negative.
- Review your credit report on a regular basis and check it for accuracy. Report any negative inaccuracies that you find to the credit bureaus. Each credit bureau must supply you with one free copy of your credit report annually. You can request these at www.annualcreditreport.com.

Stone #7: Insurance Review

Let's refer back to your personal balance sheet again. You started out by listing everything you own—all your assets. On that list are things like your car, your home, and your personal belongings. Think of all the contents of your home or apartment, and all your savings and investments. You're likely required to insure your car and your home if you own one. Yet there is a huge difference between the minimum amount of insurance you are required to have and the optimal amount of coverage for you. Failure to understand this difference could be very costly.

You'll come to understand this at the very worst time, when your car is involved in an accident or your home is damaged in a fire or storm. Get your insurance coverage reviewed now. Evaluate the risks to your assets. Seek to understand which risks are covered and which aren't. How does this apply to your investments? Some investments are insured, others aren't. Do you understand the risks you have assumed with each of your investments? Having a trusted insurance agent and a financial planner can go a long way in managing your financial risk.

This topic of insurance would not be complete without a short discussion of insuring ourselves. Typical types of coverage include health, dental, and vision. Health insurance is the most expensive and most often has the largest impact on your financial wellness.

There is a large spread among available health insurance plans. Most people have a choice of plan, whether through their employer or a public exchange. Take some time to fully understand how each plan works and determine whether it fits you. Develop a solid understanding of deductibles and out-of-pocket maximums. If something happens, will you be able to cover the costs that aren't covered by your chosen plan? Make your decisions with care and knowledge, because having the right plan is important to your physical health and your financial wellness.

Stone #8: Estate Plan

Your first reaction to the words "estate plan" is likely one of discomfort. An estate plan can be synonymous with the end of life, a topic few find pleasant. Yet as unpleasant as it may seem, not having an estate plan is far more unpleasant and stressful. Here again, obtaining the assistance of a professional is well worth the cost.

Your financial estate plan will include such items as a will, health care proxy, and power of attorney. Topics including life insurance, disability insurance, and long-term care will likely be addressed by your estate plan. Don't be thinking of this as morbid because it gets into planning for the eventuality of your death or the death of a spouse. It is actually not about death but about life: yours and that of those you love. Estate plans cover events like inability to work. How would your family be taken care of? With longer lifespans, planning for our golden years when we may not be able to fully take care of ourselves is an increasingly important topic. How and where you will live in such a situation should be very important to you. Stop equating your estate plan with dying. Associate it with living.

Financial Tip

Time can be both your friend and your foe. Regardless of your age or years to retirement, the best time to address your finances is now. Do not delay. There will never be a better day than today.

Reaching Financial Wellness

The more you incorporate the eight stepping-stones into your life, the less financial stress you will have. Financial wellness is about living life well. Your finances are a very important variable in your personal equation. It is a variable that will either propel you to the life you desire or hold you back and tie your hands, keeping you from implementing change. Again, don't focus on being rich or on mistakes of the past that have kept your financial wellness from being where you want it is to be. Break through your financial roadblocks and take advantage of new opportunities that will lead toward your ideal future.

■ Our Story: Financial Peace

People who know us personally see us as a close-knit couple. Here is a big part of our secret: implementing the eight stepping-stones has minimized our financial stress and allowed us to be so much more cohesive. Simply put, we never fight over money. Truly, we just don't. If there is something we need or want—something one of us feels strongly about—we work together to determine the best approach. Fighting isn't an option, especially in financial discussions, as it doesn't get us anywhere except hurt. It is the last thing either one of us wants to feel and certainly doesn't help the decision-making process. As you will soon read, this approach started as we were preparing for married life.

Let's step back in time to a couple months before our wedding day. We were trying to build a vision of our married life. There were so many things to determine and questions to be answered. These plans included where we would live and what type of house we would buy. Up to that point, we had both been financially independent, with separate incomes, expenses, savings, and debts. We wondered how to make it all work without suffering many of the financial pitfalls that plagued so many other couples.

Not surprisingly, we started right with our first stepping-stone: developing a budget. Though we didn't know a lot of the details of what life would soon be like, we could get clarity around our financial situation as it stood. We agreed to build a budget and quickly realized we weren't sure where we spent our money. So what did we do? For a month, we recorded every expenditure. At the end of that month, it was easy to compile the information into a budget that addressed our unique as well as shared perspectives. It served us well and led us to make sound financial choices as newlyweds.

Ultimately, we purchased our first home, furniture, our first vehicle together, and many more things. Suffice it to say, having that budget already built allowed us to make great choices as we began our life together. We still look back at these choices and realize how well they have served us. Even when we meet with our own personal financial advisers, they are surprised at how well we have lined everything up. Apparently it is a rare occurrence, yet we contend it is a crucial component of the joy in our life.

Ultimately, we view this as a very important lesson, and it is one we have shared with many people, including college students, people we mentor, and even some of our coaching clients. The more we can help people to understand the need for these financial stepping-stones, the more we can help them get started. We hope that you will also choose to go down the path of the eight stepping-stones, achieve financial wellness, and move closer to your own ideal future.

CHAPTER 13

Climb the Belief Ladder to Find Your Sense of Purpose

Have you ever seen the daredevils who walk tightropes across canyons, waterfalls, or even skyscrapers? Something within them says to step out on the wire, and they know they will make it to the other side. They have a confidence that isn't arrogant, and many times they don't even view themselves as daredevils. This is just something they do. It seems so extraordinary that these tightrope walkers can accomplish these feats while some people fear climbing a ladder.

What makes them so different that they are willing to take such risks? They believe in themselves. They believe in their equipment. They believe in their support team. Some have even publically stated just how much they believe in a higher power. As a personal leader, one who is striving for an ideal future, you too must allow yourself to believe.

Unlike the tightrope walkers, many people are locked in a trench of self-doubt, self-deprecation, and cynicism. Being trapped in this mind-set doesn't allow the development of a personal sense of purpose. The sense of purpose, which stems from our beliefs, will guide us to where we need to let ourselves go. It allows the broader perspective of the higher power of faith, hope, and love to shine through. While not everything you want in life may be obtainable, consider how little you will achieve if you don't even try to believe it is possible.

As a personal leader, the last thing you should do is allow yourself to be mired in a trench that doesn't offer a view of what is truly possible. It would become a roadblock to your ideal future. Leaders lead themselves and others by having a view of where they can go. Now, we don't expect you to walk a tightrope, but we do want you to reach new heights. To help you along the way, we are going to offer you a ladder as a means to free yourself from this trench so that you too can find your view. Each rung of the ladder will bring you a step closer to the power of believing and to fulfilling your sense of purpose. As you climb higher and higher, your vantage point will become broader, and the horizon will fill with possibilities. You will find the freedom needed to believe.

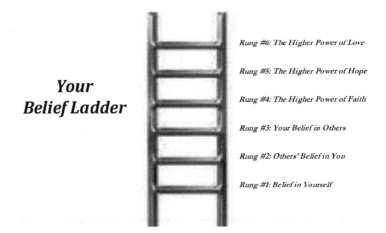

Your Belief Ladder

Rung #6: The Higher Power of Love

Rung #5: The Higher Power of Hope

Rung #4: The Higher Power of Faith

Rung #3: Your Belief in Others

Rung #2: Others' Belief in You

Rung #1: Belief in Yourself

▓▓ Climbing the Belief Ladder

The idea of the ladder is that each rung helps you to build on a different aspect of belief. The first three rungs build your confidence in yourself as well as others. Moving up to the top three rungs, you can clearly see the broader perspective of what might be, including possibilities from a higher power. Every new rung brings a better view of the three great gifts the heavens offer us: faith, hope, and love. Each is a powerful belief unto itself. Accepting these gifts and sharing them with others will lift you above what keeps so many mired in their lives. As change agents, they empower you to achieve your ideal future. It time to climb the ladder and leave the trench behind.

Rung #1: Belief in Yourself

Belief is an essential variable in your equation; without it, you will fail. As tightrope walkers make that first step out onto the wire, they know better than anyone the danger that lies in every movement they make, yet they also realize the positive possibilities. They have the confidence to defy the odds and reach the other side. If they didn't believe they were capable of success, they would never have even attempted the first step. That is the essence of belief: being able to realize the possibilities within yourself.

If we take our cue from the tightrope walkers, we will rely on our abilities and talents as the way to open the door to success. It is very hard to succeed when we don't believe it is even possible. As this is the first rung of the ladder we are building, it will be much more difficult to make it up the other steps if we don't first believe in ourselves. Our responsibility is to be in control of our own self-confidence.

All too often, we try to skip this stage, because quite frankly it can be very challenging to think differently. Unfortunately, the common expression "we are our own worst critics" holds true for most of us. The irony is that we are the only ones who have total control over our own thoughts, and we must actively choose to be our own champions. When faced with life's challenges, we should give ourselves permission to believe our positive attributes will help us through rather than thinking the negatives will just cause us to fail.

> *Be careful how you are talking to yourself because you are listening.*
> —Lisa M. Hayes

The balance between positive and negative goes back to what we learned in chapter 11. Remember—you cannot have a positive and a negative thought at the same time. When you don't believe in yourself, you're filling your head with predetermined failure. Before you even lift a finger or start to do anything, you have determined the outcome. Why would you do that to yourself?

So you might not be able make Grandma's secret-recipe pie perfectly. If you at least try, you might come up with a new version that is equally as good or even better in its own way. The point is, you had the confidence to make the attempt. You went into action with all your best efforts and intentions. Who's to say that isn't success unto itself?

Rung #2: Others' Belief in You

While a large part of tightrope walkers' success comes from their skill on the wire, an equally important part is their ability to share their stories. When tightrope walkers put on a show, often they will talk about the work they have put into the attempt and who has helped them along the way. Their story and the feat they undertake draw people in so that the audience cares and almost becomes personally involved. In much the same way, you have to understand the importance of having others around you to believe in you and your abilities.

As we discussed in chapter 10 about branding, your image and how you try to portray yourself is most certainly up to you. But you will never reach your ideal future without the help of others. Therefore, enlisting others' help by increasing their belief in you is a powerful change agent. It is up to you to determine who you should promote to and how.

For example, think about how you should brand yourself to your managers at work, certain coworkers, peers in the industry, and desirable organizations. You must promote yourself to those best positioned to help or support you in some way. If this sounds a little mercenary, it is. There are people who can provide assistance to you; however, unless you actively engage them, they may never know your name, let alone who you are and the value you can bring. Until other people truly believe in you, you won't get the kind of help and engagement you need to achieve your ideal future.

While it is extremely important to seek these engagements, it is critical to avoid pitfalls that will completely thwart your efforts. The key is to find the right balance. Under-promoting or even being self-effacing is just as damaging as bragging and boasting. We often see examples of people undertaking this crucial responsibility and doing it incorrectly. The end result is that more damage than good is done. Don't make the same mistake.

Let's get back to our tightrope-walking analogy. The tightrope walker must balance carefully, not leaning too far to the left or too far to the right. You too must balance your self-promotion carefully, walking a fine line. On the left side of the spectrum are self-deprecating behaviors. Don't put yourself down all the time, even in a joking manner, because it will become your brand. Modesty and humility are wonderful things. Too much of either devalues and belittles you, and others will think less of you for it. On the right side of the spectrum is arrogance. Constant boasting, especially without recognizing others who might have helped or worse yet without showing interest in others' lives, will push people away. Either extreme will keep you from climbing the ladder. Your goal is to walk right down the middle of the spectrum. You'll maximize the belief that others have in you and all the support they might provide.

Rung #3: Your Belief in Others

Our tightrope walker wouldn't be very confident without a trusted support team to manage every detail and ensure a successful walk over that wire. Just as you need others to believe in you, it is equally important for you to believe in others. You can view others in two ways: The first is with cynicism, assuming that everyone is out to take care of his or her own interests. The second, which should be more desirable, is to view people as trustworthy and benevolent, doing good deeds for others. Hint: the cynical view won't get you to your ideal future.

Now step back and take a hard look at yourself. Are you sure you aren't cynical? Another way to look at this is to ask yourself whether you view most people as generally trustworthy. If your answer is that people shouldn't be trusted and you aren't in the habit of extending trust to others, you're likely suffering from cynicism. Abolish that now; no good will come from it. It will be a bigger roadblock than you may think. Instead, seek to find the positives in others. Your goal should be to build trusting relationships whenever possible. Extend trust willingly and then modify as necessary. Without these relationships, you are an army of one. With them, you are an army of many, all interdependent.

Now take some initiative and take action. Nothing is ever going to change if you don't make the first move. Invite some people out, strike up some conversations, allow yourself to be vulnerable, and get to know them. The sense of openness will be received and reciprocated. Together you will help each other up the ladder.

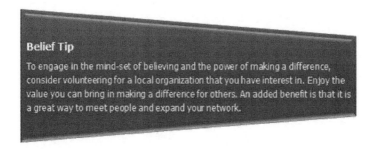

Belief Tip

To engage in the mind-set of believing and the power of making a difference, consider volunteering for a local organization that you have interest in. Enjoy the value you can bring in making a difference for others. An added benefit is that it is a great way to meet people and expand your network.

Rung #4: The Higher Power of Faith

Faith can have a couple of different interpretations. In general, faith is a deep and complete belief in something without having every detail or absolute proof. The other, religious interpretation is the belief in a higher power. Faith, religious or secular, can be a powerful change agent. While we are choosing to be candid about our Christian faith, our intent is not to prescribe any religious view but to raise the topic as something that deserves careful and thoughtful consideration.

Faith is available to all, and it doesn't require one to subscribe to an organized religion. In his book *Keeping the Faith Without a Religion*, Roger Housden explains how faith is a gift for everyone. Housden states that faith may or may not include the sense of a personal God or an afterlife: "Faith refers to a matter not of the head but the heart. It implies an orientation of trust and love-for-no-reason. Just because."[11] Prayer may be replaced by meditation and contemplation and perhaps by even simpler things like taking a walk in a park—whatever puts us in connection with ourselves and ultimately allows us a connection to a world without the need to have proof of every detail. That's the true essence of faith.

Personally, our faith in God has brought us through many difficult trials. We are confident in our faith and have experienced its ability to create change. The power of prayer is a change agent we highly recommend to everyone. You have likely found yourself in situations, perhaps desperate situations, where you felt powerless to make an impact. These are often the exact type of situations where many people will turn to prayer. Our view is that we are never powerless if we are able to pray. The quiet contemplation and reflection associated with prayer can open our minds and free our hearts. The irony of this change agent is that most people who have prayer in their lives have prayed for change.

Our suggestion is to make a date with yourself and devote it to some reflection and prayer as to where faith fits in your life. Faith is a wonderful gift available to us all. It's a gift as big as you want to make it. Only you can decide.

Rung #5: The Higher Power of Hope

Often in life, we receive an outcome that isn't quite what we expected. Yet somehow it does seem to work out for the best. Without hope, we lose the chance for a best outcome. If you don't hope for the best, you likely assume the worst. This negative mindset makes it very likely that you will receive just that, because you have lost the perspective of what might be. Why devote any energy or effort to something where there is no hope for success?

While hope doesn't assure a specific outcome, lack of hope almost always assures a negative result. Hope is something entirely within your control. You can create and hold on to it, or you can give it up. Have you given up hope on a number of things? It's time to take another look at these and rethink. Hope, like faith, is a powerful gift that only you can decide when and how to harness to change your equation.

Rung #6: The Higher Power of Love

If you were to ask tightrope walkers why they do it, they would probably tell you they love it. The feeling of being so high above everything, the grand view of the world, and even the thrill of the feat all amount to love for them. They use the love they feel on the wire to pursue their goals.

Love is often referred to as God's greatest gift to man. In the perspective of personal leadership, love is much broader than romantic feelings. Love has a great power to create change as it engages people and unites them. It is said that love is a gift, and unlike faith and hope, it must be shared to capture its power. While you can harness much of the power of faith and hope by keeping it for yourself, love is meant to be given away to others. Understanding this concept is essential to unwrapping this gift.

Now that you're standing on the highest rung of the ladder, you can see more with greater perspective. While love can be experienced in infinite forms, there is only one way to maximize the gift: share it without expectation. Love shared with others without expectation of receiving anything in return is loving in the highest form. Expecting something in return reduces an act of love to a simple business transaction between two parties.

Give of yourself. You will only truly experience love's full power by sharing it unconditionally. You have so much to share with the world; share your knowledge, your experiences, and everything else you have. Do it with love, and you will grow the love you have in your life. It truly is fitting that love is the pinnacle of our climb.

▩ Roe's Ladder of Beliefs

Over the past decade or so, I have been blessed with an incredible life—a wonderful marriage, an immediate family that grows stronger and closer, the development of a fulfilling career, and a call to my true purpose. Even my beloved little dog, Pixie, is an incredible joy to me. Sure, even to this day there are rough patches in life to face. Yes, there are more things I would like to accomplish in life. Overall, however, if anyone asks about my life, overwhelmingly my answer is usually, "I am blessed."

I have developed such a sense of gratitude to my faith and to God that I have found myself sharing my blessings as much as possible with others. It is a theme within my family, especially with my mom, and it really has spoken to my own sense of purpose. My way of thanking God and the heavens above for such a blessed life is to make sure I try to do the same for others. My personal ladder of beliefs has led me to understand that true fulfillment comes in part from helping others in their lives.

The more I progress along life's journey, the more this truly becomes apparent. A few years ago, I was waiting at a restaurant bar for a friend to join me for dinner. An older man asked if I knew what my purpose in life was. He was a college professor and liked to challenge people with that question. He was the one who wound up surprised, though, when I said, "Yes, in fact I do know what it is. I am a fairy godmother sent to help people around me."

While you might be chuckling to yourself, please know this: it's true, and people who know me often hear me say it. As a fairy godmother, my mission is to bring the blessings and joy I have in my life to those God sends to me for help. The best part is that this sense of purpose is now shared by Don. He is always beside me, encouraging, supporting, and often even financing these gifting moments.

A great example of this came recently. Don and I went to a fast food restaurant for a quick lunch. The girl behind the counter had glasses that were so horribly broken that she even tried to glue the lenses herself in an attempt to fix them. Don and I both have terrible vision, so we could empathize with her. After we left that day, I was really troubled by this for a couple of weeks. My fairy godmother instinct was on full alert—so much so that I warned Don when we went back that if the girl still had broken glasses, we were going to do something.

Well, sure enough, when we went back the situation was worse than expected. She was trying to live without the glasses entirely and was continually squinting and struggling with even the simplest of tasks. Without hesitation, we called her over to our table, and Don gave her money to go to an eye-care store I found for her. Our mutual sense of purpose was fulfilled when she took the money. We have gone back, and she is always excited to see us—plus she looks great in her new glasses.

Our gestures aren't always so profound. They might include a shopping trip for someone who needs clothes, an extra donation to the church for a nun who would like to help the shut-ins, or maybe just treating someone I am coaching to an open, caring conversation over lunch. In any event, I take my ladder and I try to help others climb out of the situations they have found themselves in. The true belief in myself and my purpose comes from the look of relief I see when I tell them that I am a fairy godmother and I am there to help.

Usually somehow, some way, even if it is only for a little while, the recipient finds peace and a sense of hope. It has brought me such joy to share this sense of purpose with others. From the bottom of my heart, I ask that you take inspiration from my own mission and build your ladder to find your own sense of purpose. When you truly believe, miracles really do happen.

CHAPTER 14

Live Your Legacy Now

There is a huge difference between simply leaving something behind and giving the world exactly the gifts you intended. Your legacy should be founded on intentions: your intentions. Should it be your intention to simply leave behind what you have left over from your life, money, and material possessions? Would it not be better to be proactive and have the intention to gift yourself to the world as you live each day?

As you answer these questions, legacy actually becomes a change agent, but this is unique in that you can use all the other factors to create it. Managing your legacy allows you to fully understand the course you set for yourself and how you will be able to view your life when it is time to leave it.

When people have meaning, people have joy. Think about the life you will live as your legacy; it's not just what you will leave behind. A legacy is about you, those close to you, and even your impact on the greater world.

All too often, people don't have joy because they are so obsessed with what they don't have. They don't have the house they want, the car they want, or any of the material possessions they hope to obtain when they win that lottery. Other times, people lack clarity in their life, so they spend their time constantly searching for the next job, the next home, and the next new thing. What they are really searching for is their reason for being. Personally, we have seen so many people without purpose, mission, or joy. All too often they are just so lost that their unhappiness shines through for the world to see. They are going through the motions of life without fully embracing the true value of it. Their focus is in the wrong direction.

The complete joy of reaching an ideal future isn't about accumulating everything you want in the world. Part of that joy actually comes from maximizing your gifts to the world. Your sense of purpose has moved beyond the inward focus and is now outward toward the life you live now and the legacy it will create.

This newfound enjoyment of life will be sensed by those closest to you and will positively impact them. Your legacy is something to be lived, and in doing so you'll leave behind exactly what you intended. By living your legacy now, you will enrich your life and the lives of those around you. Enrichment is the sum of this book; it is your life's equation. You are finding the meaning and purpose to reach your ideal future.

> *Legacy is not leaving something for people,*
> *it's leaving something in people.*
> *—Peter Strople*

▨ How We Started to Live Our Legacy

Living our own legacy was not something we ever meant to do. Like many, many others, we worked, studied, and tried to live our lives acquiring what we thought we wanted. Unlike so many others, from our earliest days of dating we had goals and even our dream days.

As life progressed, we did end up in some battles over which direction we should take. There were times we were mired in the stress of not knowing what would be the right decision to bring us fulfillment. Then a few things happened that changed our lives in ways we'd never imagined were possible.

One of those life-changing events arose somewhat out of the blue. We were witnessing a situation play out over the course of a few months with a family we were introduced to but didn't know very well. They were dealing with a level of poverty we have never personally experienced. Sure, there were times in our lives when money was tight and we had to do without, but that never meant going without food or being in imminent danger of losing a job because of a lack of reliable transportation like this family was facing. So, needless to say, as we began to understand just how dire some people's circumstances could be, we became aware of how bad life would turn out for this family if we didn't step in to help.

They were trapped in an upside-down car loan in which the dealer preyed upon their poverty. Now there were so many car repair bills and absences from work that the downward spiral was increasing with no way out. With rising debts and missed work, the family would never get out from under the crushing debt or even be able to put food on the table. They needed help. They needed us.

The act of stepping in was disconcerting. Sure we had helped others, but never like this, and several of our advisers even warned us against doing it. There were moments of doubt and conflicted feelings as we faced the prospect. In the end, the situation continued to deteriorate, so we decided we would have to put our reservations aside, be brave, and approach this family with an offer of help. We needed to get them out of the spiral and into a solid, reliable vehicle for their future. It would cost a considerable amount of money to do this, and yet if we didn't, the family would literally sink into a level of poverty from which there was no foreseeable escape.

Please know, the family didn't ask us for help. It never crossed their minds that relative strangers would do such a thing. However, they didn't refuse us either when we told them we were going to get them out of this situation. We spent time understanding the issues with the existing car and loan. We spent time with them going from dealer to dealer searching for the best options available. We ended up spending more money than we'd planned, but we made sacrifices of our time and money without question. We did have to change priorities regarding our ideal future, such as some home improvements we had been planning for that had to be put off, yet we did it without question. It was just the right thing to do.

Over time, as the full impact of our help came to fruition, we experienced a personal joy that we hadn't known was even possible. The family has flourished, and now they are an active part of our lives. We changed more priorities, offered more help to more people, and much to our surprise, our joy continued to grow. This gradually shifted our focus, which now includes gifting ourselves to others. In one of the more special gifting moments, we evoked such tears of joy and gratitude that we ended up experiencing them ourselves. It was a double win and one we will never, ever forget.

In the end, we weren't looking to be fairy godparents, yet it has become a role we cherish. Even more importantly, we truly cherish those who have joined our lives because of it. We have shifted priorities and added much to the vision of our ideal future because of our developing mission. Part of that shift is this book, which is our contribution to you and anyone else who may be searching for an ideal future.

▪ Developing Your Legacy

Believing in yourself is a step toward developing a personal mission. Embracing your personal mission will help you to build the legacy you want, not just the one you assume by default. Because the legacy starts with a mission, you need to articulate your mission statement. This involves writing down your thoughts in a few sentences.

Stephen R. Covey, author of *The 7 Habits of Highly Effective People*, defines a personal mission statement as something that "focuses on what you want to be (character) and to do (contributions and achievements) and on the values or principles upon which being and doing are based."[12] An example could be something like this: "I will be an assistant for those in need, helping them reach their potential." A personal mission isn't something that is created overnight. It takes time, talent, and resources to truly find the right way. It takes your life's equation.

Once you employ your mission and develop an understanding that your legacy is something to be lived each and every day, your priorities in life become evident. Where you have been struggling to decide among various choices, suddenly the decisions become less stressful. Your mission will become your compass pointing you in the direction of your ideal future.

Life Elements + The Realities + Change Agents = **IDEAL FUTURE**

CHAPTER 15

Your Ideal Future

Throughout this book, we have pushed you to look inward at your life elements, realities, and change agents. In the end, however, changing your equation comes down to not only finding the joy, meaning, and purpose in your life but also activating it and putting it into real action.

In identifying and striving for your ideal future, you will come to realize that the promises of life need to be fulfilled. Repeat these statements to yourself and know they are true:

1. There is no reason for me to abandon hopes and dreams.
2. There is no reason for me to just live day to day.
3. There is no reason I should look at my life and wonder why I am even here.

All the factors in your equation this book has outlined constitute embracing the opportunities life puts before you. There are occasions when you will be able to serve yourself, to serve others, and to serve the world. When these possibilities are realized, a sense of purpose will emerge. The more you accomplish, the clearer your true mission will become. From this growing sense of purpose and mission, you will experience true joy in life. The factors we have shown in this book will help you reach that ideal future.

◼ Life Elements

Life elements are the foundation of who we are. Everyone has them. Collectively, they constitute the starting point. We need to understand relationships, values and ethics, education, finances, and our careers so we can set a course for our ideal future. Inventorying these key categories will make life's circumstances clearer.

◼ The Realities

The realities of you as a person, of others around you, and of a leader's world are the three categories we looked at in this factor. Our focus was on creating a realistic perspective of what is truly achievable. While we encourage everyone to dream big, an ideal future isn't a dream. It's a reality that you can achieve.

◼ Change Agents

Change agents are the final set of factors. They include being an entrepreneur and setting your own direction; knowing how the brand you have works for you or against you; choosing the current of growth and defeating the trap of negative thinking; following the stepping-stones to financial wellness; understanding the role of beliefs and the ladder needed to reach a higher perspective; and defining the legacy you live for your ideal future. Hidden in these change agents are roadblocks to our success. When we stop to analyze these categories, we can see the roadblocks and remove them, as the invisible becomes visible.

▓ Completing the Vision of Your Ideal Future

As your sense of purpose becomes clearer and you have more definition of what your personal mission should be and how these change agents can affect that mission, the next step is to go back to the vision of your ideal future. When you created the list, the focus was probably inward. It is your life, after all, and all along we have been saying that you're allowed to reach your goals. This is still very true; however, now we want to challenge you to take it one step further. How does your ideal future offer a balance of give and take?

An ideal future that is solely focused on personal needs and wants probably won't bring the desired results. If we only aspire to accumulate everything we desire, we will not find the sense of personal satisfaction that comes with the ideal future. If we only gift everything we have, we will still not achieve that sense. Only in finding the right balance for ourselves will we find the right balance for our ideal future.

Determining how much to give versus how much to keep is not a trivial feat. It is a decision that needs to be made so that you're living in such a way that both personal wants and the ability to serve others are achieved. A good place to start is to do a review of your vision for an ideal future. For each item, ask yourself if it supports or detracts from your mission. As you go through the list, make notes, because it is likely you will experience some important revelations.

The development of your mission might mean that you will need to reprioritize some of your wants. Perhaps you'll trade out some of the items you hope to acquire for gifts you would rather offer instead. Maybe you will come to the realization that the expensive sports car you've had your eye on is better replaced by a lesser car or that you're willing to wait longer for it. This short-term savings will allow you to help others in their needs. In the end, your sacrifice furthers your mission and ultimately your legacy.

Life will always hand you a large number of decisions. There is no escaping them. When you know your purpose—your ideal future—the answers to life's dilemmas will be clearer. And as we mentioned earlier, the ideal future may change as you change, as your priorities and mission become more refined. Use the tools in this book to get you to your new destination. But always make sure you try to enjoy the journey to your amazing ideal future.

Acknowledgments

When we first set out on the journey of writing a book, we had no comprehension of just what a journey it would be. As we told more people of our aspiration, we were overwhelmed by the responses of encouragement, experience, support, and even love. We are truly grateful for all of you, especially those listed here.

First and foremost, we acknowledge each other. We accomplished something not many married couples could, and it was an absolute joy! We debated, discussed, and even laughed through this process. It was a true joy to work, learn, and grow together. This was a joint success, even before the first copy was published.

We thank God for the blessings He has abundantly provided in our lives. His guidance was ever present in this process, and we look forward to continuing to serve Him in the future.

Of course, loving thanks goes out to our families, especially Roe's dad and mom, John and Janice Lucadamo, and sister, Susan Bartkowiak; and Don's aunt, Jane Godlewski. Your calls and check-ins were so encouraging and supportive of this process that it bolstered our confidence to succeed and the need to keep working toward our goal.

To our dear friends, especially Julie Kritzler, and those whom we could not socialize with as much because we were working, thank you. Again, your encouragement and support were wonderful.

For our "fairy godchildren," thank you so much for the inspiration. By allowing us to contribute to your lives, you have greatly inspired our lives.

In these acknowledgments, we also want to recognize our business relationships—Larry Gilroy, owner of Gilroy, Kernan, and Gilroy, and the teams there that support Don in his professional career, as well as Roe's clients, all of whom have had a profound impact on our professional lives. We are grateful.

Special thanks to our own personal mentors and coaches, especially Larry Linne, who was generous in sharing his time and the knowledge we needed to see this through to publication, and Mark Amtower, whose vision for how we can share this work has been a godsend. Your belief in us and our potential are truly gifts you have given of yourselves. And finally, very special acknowledgment to Kathi Wittkamper, editorial consultant at iUniverse, and Adam Lawless and the MPW Marketing team. You were the final thread we needed to make this dream a reality.

References

1. Tom Rath, *Strengths Finder 2.0* (New York: Gallup Press, 2007).
2. Steve Farber, *Greater Than Yourself: The Ultimate Lesson of True Leadership* (New York: Doubleday, 2009), 3.
3. Lee Brower, *The Brower Quadrant: Live Life Deliberately* (New York: L. Brower, 2009), 117.
4. Larry G. Linne and Patrick Sitkins, *Brand Aid: Taking Control of Your Reputation—Before Everyone Else Does* (New York: Penguin Group, 2014), 19.
5. Rhonda Byrne, *The Secret* (New York: Atria Books, 2006), 16–17.
6. Judith Orloff, MD, "Intuitive Strategies to Stop Taking on Other People's Stress and Negativity" and "Intuition, Empath Support, Traditional and Alternative Medicine, Emotions and Energy Healing" (March 2, 2008), accessed May 30, 2016, http://drjudithorloff.com/.
7. David Bach, *The Automatic Millionaire: A Powerful One-Step Plan to Live and Finish Rich* (New York: Broadway Books, 2004).
8. Ramit Sethi, *I Will Teach You to Be Rich* (New York: Workman Publishing, 2009).
9. Daniel C. Goldie and Gordon S. Murray, *The Investment Answer: Learn to Manage Your Money and Protect Your Financial Future* (New York: Business Plus, 2011).
10. Ken Sweet and Emily Swanson, "Poll: Two-Thirds of US Would Struggle to Cover $1,000 Crisis" (May 19, 2016), accessed May 25, 2016, http://www.apnorc.org/news-media/Pages/News Media/Poll -Two-thirds-of-US-would-struggle-to-cover-$1,000-crisis.aspx.
11. Roger Housden, *Keeping the Faith Without a Religion*, Kindle edition, location 184.
12. Stephen R. Covey, *The 7 Habits of Highly Effective People: Powerful Lessons in Personal Change* (New York: Fireside Press, 1989), 106.

Made in the USA
Middletown, DE
03 April 2017